80p

D1585167

The Work of the Queen

QUEEN ELIZABETH II

[Armstrong Jones

THE WORK
OF THE QUEEN

by

DERMOT MORRAH

Arundel Herald Extraordinary
Late Fellow of All Souls College, Oxford

WILLIAM KIMBER
LONDON

First published in 1958 by
WILLIAM KIMBER AND CO. LIMITED
46 Wilton Place, London, S.W.1

© William Kimber and Co. Limited 1958

MADE AND PRINTED IN GREAT BRITAIN BY PURNELL AND SONS, LTD.
PAULTON (SOMERSET) AND LONDON

Acknowledgements

The Privy Purse entrance to Buckingham Palace leads to a long corridor from which opens on the right-hand side a series of quiet dignified apartments. Each is occupied by one of the private secretaries or other confidential servants of the Queen or the Duke of Edinburgh. It is possibly the most important duty of these dedicated men and women to keep open the lines of communication between the Queen and her subjects, both by bringing to her aid all who have anything to contribute to her limitless function as universal representative of the entire British Commonwealth of Nations, and by helping to keep her personality present and vivid to the minds of all her peoples. Among more important aspects of this duty of communication, they are always ready to prompt, to guide and to correct those who endeavour to interpret the monarchy in print. Once satisfied that the inquirer comes with faith in the institution of the Throne and loyalty to the person of the Queen, there are no bounds to the patience, courtesy and consideration they will show him; and their frankness extends to the utmost limit that the confidential character of their employment will allow.

These men and women desire no publicity for themselves and none will be given to them in the chapters that follow. Scarcely a page, however, could have been written without continual recourse to their information and advice. Of those who have helped me since I began this present work I should like to record special gratitude to Sir Michael Adeane, Sir Edward Ford, Lt.-Col. The Hon. Martin Charteris, Commander Richard Colville, Miss Anthea Fairfax-Ross and (in the Lord Chamberlain's Office) Sir Terence Nugent; but if I have any understanding of the

Acknowledgements

operation of the monarchy, it owes quite as much to the friendship and guidance others, their predecessors in the Household,
have extended to me from far back in the reign of George VI.

Some of the substance of the second chapter has already appeared in *Berlingske Tidende*, of Copenhagen, and some paragraphs
of the last in the *Navy Year Book* for 1955. I am grateful to the
two Editors for permission to reprint them.

Contents

The Preparation

The Preparation

THE first child of Albert Duke of York and his wife, formerly Lady Elizabeth Bowes-Lyon, was born at 17 Bruton Street, London, the home of the Duchess's parents, Lord and Lady Strathmore, on April 21, 1926. Five weeks later she was baptized by Cosmo Lang, Archbishop of York, in the name of Elizabeth Alexandra Mary, after her mother, grandmother and great-grandmother. As a daughter of the King's son she enjoyed princely rank by right of birth, and was therefore formally known at once as Her Royal Highness the Princess Elizabeth of York. She was the first grandchild of King George V to have this status; for her elder cousin, Lord Lascelles, son of the Princess Royal, was not entitled to it, being of the female line; nor indeed did he stand within measurable distance of the succession, for all the King's four sons, and all children who might be born to them, would have preference over his mother and him.

The newborn Princess was therefore from the first a public figure. It was many years since there had been a nursery associated with the royal palaces. Her birth meant that there were now three generations of human beings to support the Throne, and was widely hailed, in a troubled and anxious phase of the national history, as an augury for the future. It is commonly said that in Princess Elizabeth's childhood nobody thought of her as a future Queen. There is some truth in this, but it should not be exaggerated. At the time of the Princess's birth the King was 61. Edward Prince of Wales was nearly 32. He had been given opportunities to meet all the eligible princesses of Europe, and the unmarried daughters of

11

the most honoured English and Scottish families. Though he sometimes spoke with good-natured envy of the happiness his younger brother had found in marriage, his lack of personal interest in any of the young ladies who had been so carefully brought to his notice was becoming conspicuous.

The possibility that the reign of George V would never see a Princess of Wales was being openly discussed, and to many, including some very close to the Royal Family, it was beginning to seem a probability. Sooner or later, in the natural course, some member of the generation younger than the Prince of Wales must wear the Crown. If it were not to be a son or daughter of the Prince, then it would be a child of the Duke of York. It already seemed more likely that the little Princess would eventually be displaced from the succession by a brother of her own than by a child of her uncle's. But for the time being she had to be regarded as the first royal representative of the nursery generation until another child, standing nearer to the succession, should be born. No such child ever was. Thus the idea that Princess Elizabeth of York would one day be Queen Elizabeth II was never altogether remote from the thoughts of her family or her future subjects. Imperceptibly as the years went by it changed from a curious speculation to a possibility and then to a probability. It is impossible to assign critical dates to any stage of the process, or to identify the moment when it was realized to be a certainty. It has very little to do with the accession of her father to the Throne, for before that time it was generally accepted that the Princess was destined to come next after the two elder sons of George V. Whether one or both of them was to reign before her made little difference; it was natural to suppose that she would become Queen, as a middle-aged or elderly woman, when both were gone.

Thus from the very first Princess Elizabeth had a unique position as a symbol of things to come, and even in infancy was bound to be the target of an overwhelming public curiosity, which would have shifted its aim if a nearer heir had been born, but which as it turned out was never withdrawn until the day she was called to the Throne. That year contained two other pointers to the future. In the first place, it was the date of the famous Imperial Conference at which the Balfour Declaration was adopted, setting forth the constitutional equality of all the nations of the British Commonwealth. When thrown into formal shape in the Statute of Westminster five years later, this doctrine had the effect of cutting all links of legal compulsion between the members of the Commonwealth, leaving their common allegiance to the Throne as their only visible bond. Thus it was known—though not to a baby princess—that every successor of George V would be called upon to play a double part, both as the head or father of each sovereign member of the Commonwealth separately, and as the symbol of unity for the greater whole of which they were all parts.

Secondly, 1926 was the year in which the social discontents of the post-war epoch in Great Britain came to a head in the general strike, which broke out before Princess Elizabeth was ten days old. The odious spirit of class-war, so foreign to the British tradition, came nearer to prevailing in those days than at any time before or since; and there followed the bitter years of unemployment and financial collapse, on which all who held authority in those times look back with shame, and for which all political parties would like to shift the responsibility upon one another. It was a time that called especially for the healing power of the monarchy as the universal representative, the symbol of social cohesion across the barriers of class; and a great share of the task of closing the ranks was assumed by the Duke of York.

He tried to establish the sense of brotherhood in the future leaders of the nation by bringing the young sons of rich and poor families together in his annual summer camps; he was assiduous in making himself personally acquainted with the

13

people in their working places at the factory bench or in the mines, so that he came to be known as the industrial prince. All sorts and conditions of the people came to his house to consult him and the Duchess, and the atmosphere of dedication to social service provided the background of the princess's nursery and schoolroom life. The representative monarchy of the twentieth century, of which George V may be accounted the founder, was taking shape very close to her unconscious head; and though her introduction to its spirit and functions belongs to a much later stage in her growth, she could scarcely have discovered that there are some children who are not born princes and princesses before she was also half aware that in some way her life must be given to their service.

Unconsciously, she was making her first sacrifice to the duties of her public position before she was a year old; for directly after her first Christmas, which she spent with the whole Royal Family at Sandringham, she had to be parted from her father and mother, who were sailing on a high imperial mission, to preside in state over the inauguration of the new capital of the Commonwealth of Australia at Canberra. Her grandfather's subjects at the other side of the world showed themselves very conscious of her significance in the scheme of loyalty; and at the end of the tour H.M.S. *Renown* sailed from Perth with three tons of presents for Her Royal Highness in her hold—including twenty live parrots. After a small selection had been made for the toy cupboard at 145 Piccadilly, where the Duke and Duchess now had their London home, the remainder were distributed to children's hospitals—a significant illustration of the representative character of royalty even in infant days. For it was not difficult for the Australian donors to realize that in giving to the baby princess they were giving by token to children in general, and more particularly to the children whose need was greatest; and that this disposal of their gifts was the truest thanks that could be returned on her behalf.

The temporary orphan had divided her time between the homes of her four grandparents, Lord and Lady Strathmore at Glamis Castle in Scotland and St. Paul's Walden Bury in Hertfordshire, and King George and Queen Mary at Sandringham and Windsor. She became very dear to the old King; and after his grave illness at the end of 1928 it was part of his treatment in convalescence to have his little granddaughter sent to keep him company at Bognor. She was at that time not quite three years old. Before she was four the King deputed his stud groom, Owen, to teach her to ride on her first Shetland pony, called Peggy, and so introduced her to what has become her principal recreation. Sharing in the common devotion of all young children to animals, which with her access to many great country houses she had abundant opportunity to gratify, she rapidly developed a special interest in horses which was to outlive other childish hobbies.

She became an excellent horsewoman, as was much to be desired in view of the ceremonial parts she might one day have to play in the saddle; but also she became very early in life a student of form and pedigree in racing stock, including especially the royal stud, in which her father and grandfather took only a moderate interest. She was only five when, at the Duke of York's request, she was taken out with the Pytchley to be "blooded"; but there was no kill, and, though she afterwards followed the Beaufort once or twice, she never acquired much taste for fox-hunting.

On August 15, 1930, Princess Margaret was born at Glamis; and from that day onwards to that of Princess Elizabeth's wedding the two sisters, notwithstanding the difference of more than four years in age, were rarely separated. Since neither of them was to be sent away to school, the nursery phase of childhood merged rather gradually into that of formal education. Miss Knight, the nurse, who had also nursed the Duchess of York in her infancy, made way in 1933 for the first governess, Miss Marion Crawford, who was to continue at her post until lessons were outgrown. Before long other teachers were called in to give specialist help: teachers of dancing, of swimming, of music, and the Vicomtesse de Bellaigues to teach the princesses French.

Still later the Provost of Eton, Sir Henry Marten, was asked to introduce Princess Elizabeth to such branches of knowledge as were particularly required for the equipment of a future Queen. But all alike were working under authority; it was not left to any of them to determine the general direction, or even the major details, of the princesses' education. That was shaped to a clearly conceived plan, which was framed by their mother. By comparison with the curricula of the leading girls' schools of that day or this, the plan would be considered somewhat old-fashioned; indeed Queen Mary, who was by temperament more inclined than her daughter-in-law to put a high value on strictly intellectual discipline, sometimes expressed her misgivings. But the Duchess of York had a definite idea of the sort of training she wished her daughters to receive, and pursued her course untroubled by other people's doubts. She desired them first of all to spend as much of their childhood as possible in the open air, and, however much in later life they might become involved in the pomps of cities, to learn to feel always at home in country surroundings and country pursuits. Then she would have them acquire good manners and perfect deportment, and to cultivate all the distinctively feminine graces; for she is of those whose natural instinct is to emphasize the contrast between the sexes rather than seek to assimilate them to one another.

She desired them to develop a civilized appreciation of the arts, and especially of music, in which she herself has some accomplishment. After care had been taken of these elements of a young lady's all-round education, the Duchess fully agreed that her children should gain as much reasonable book-learning as might prove to be within their capacity; but this she regarded as only one of several branches of education, to be kept in proper proportion with the rest and in subordination to the whole. When, for example, it became apparent that Princess Elizabeth would never progress beyond the simplest elements of mathematics, it did not worry the Duchess at all.

From the beginning of this education, at the age of seven, Princess Elizabeth's day followed a strict routine. She got up at 7.30 and, after breakfasting in the nursery, went downstairs for a quarter of an hour with her parents. Then there were lessons from 9.15 to 11.0 and again from 11.30 to 12.30; and this, in the earliest phase, was the end of book-work for the day. The Princess always joined her parents at luncheon if they were at home; and in fine weather she invariably spent the afternoon out of doors. Music and drawing lessons were fitted in on the wet days. Tea was in the schoolroom at 4.45, and then from 5.30 the Duchess always had her children with her for an hour in her sitting-room. Bedtime for the seven-year-old was at 6.45.

This quiet timetable, with the hours spent at the desk gradually lengthening as the children grew, regulated their lives through the closing years of their grandfather's reign. Every effort was made to secure for them the normal upbringing of any children born into a comfortably situated family of private station; but it would of course be absurd to pretend that there was no difference between their life and that of ordinary little girls. "Ordinary" children do not find themselves followed by crowds of sightseers whenever they go out for a walk or peered at through the railings from the park when they play in the garden of 145 Piccadilly; they do not meet the highest personages in all spheres of public life when they come down to meals with their parents, nor do they see those parents playing solemn and decorative parts in the great ceremonies of national pageantry. What the Duke and Duchess could and did insist on was that their daughters, though necessarily conscious of their unique position among their contemporaries, should never be tempted to think of their privilege as something inherent in their own merits, but should realize that they were of one clay with the less exalted children who crossed their path and learn to mix with these on equal and easy terms. Among the sons and daughters of the Household staff at Buckingham Palace and Windsor, at the swimming club where they spent many of their afternoons, and later in the Girl Guides, they put their royal rank into abeyance and learned the arts of human intercourse.

Public appearances were restricted to the absolute minimum, but occasionally exceptions had to be made. Princess Elizabeth for example attended Princess Marina of Greece as a bridesmaid at her wedding to the Duke of Kent in November 1934, and came again to Westminster Abbey in a like capacity when the Duke of Gloucester married Lady Alice Scott. And she took her place as chief representative of the third generation of the Royal Family in the moving celebrations of the Silver Jubilee of King George and Queen Mary, sitting just behind the King in St. Paul's Cathedral, and afterwards coming out on the balcony of the Palace with her elders while her grandparents acknowledged the acclamations of thousands upon thousands of his devoted subjects, cheering for hour after hour in the open space below. Less than a year later, holding her mother's hand in St. George's Chapel at Windsor, she watched the King's coffin being lowered into the vault, while Garter King of Arms proclaimed the sonorous roll of his titles. She was then nearly ten years old—perhaps not too young to feel some of the significance of those two scenes of sunshine and shadow, so swiftly following the one upon the other, or to have some intuition of the glory and sorrow that chequer the life of kings.

King George V died on January 20, 1936. This was the year, as looking back we can see, when the turbid stream of events

that had emerged from the confusions of the Versailles Treaty
began to gather pace towards the cataract of another world war.
It was the year when Hitler marched into the Rhineland and
General Franco landed in Spain. These omens of the forces that
were to reshape her world were beyond the comprehension
of a princess ten years old. Nor was it for her to fathom the
vortex of emotions that engulfed the Royal Family in the last
weeks of the year and swept King Edward VIII from the throne
of his fathers. She only knew that her uncle David had disap-
peared across the sea; that her father and mother were moving
into Buckingham Palace and becoming invested with alarming
pomp and circumstance; and that she herself was no longer
Princess Elizabeth of York, but Princess Elizabeth of England,
heiress presumptive to the Throne.

It might have turned out quite otherwise. Since Parliament
must be asked to alter the laws of succession so as to transfer
the Crown from the heir designated by the Act of Settlement
to some other person, it was not a legal necessity that the person
selected should be the next in hereditary order; and there are
veteran officers of the Household who remember how much
persuasion had to be brought to bear upon the Duke of York
in order to persuade him that he was the man that the nation
and Empire overwhelmingly desired to see at their head.
Excessively modest though he was, he would never on his own
account have repudiated the new load of responsibility; but he
shrank from imposing the burden eventually on his daughter.
At that time the only prince near to the line of succession who
had a son was the Duke of Kent, and the draftsmen preparing
the Abdication Bill at least tentatively considered what to do if
his two elder brothers asked to stand aside in his favour. But
this was only a momentary speculation, dismissed in a few hours;
for it was rapidly apparent, not only that a great fund of popular
good will had been building up for years round the Duke and
Duchess of York, but also that the public affection for their

children had contributed very much to their popularity. The new heiress presumptive was already a public figure in her own right.

For a few months Princess Elizabeth lived constantly in the public eye, months of gathering excitement as the carpenters hammered the beams for the stands along the Mall, and the dressmakers came to Buckingham Palace to measure the children for their coronation robes. On the day—it was May 12, 1937—they walked on either side of their aunt the Princess Royal to their places in the royal gallery over the tomb of Anne of Cleves, each wearing a long train of purple velvet; and at the moment when the Archbishop set the crown of the Queen Consort on their mother's head each of them put on the coronet of a king's daughter, a gold circlet ornamented with crosses formy and fleurs-de-lis. Still in their robes they drove in the procession through the London streets and later in the day joined the crowned King and Queen on the balcony of the Palace to respond to the cheering of the mighty crowds.

After these alarums and excursions the princesses were firmly returned to the schoolroom to pass in such seclusion as could be contrived the two remaining years of uneasy peace while the thunderclouds gathered over Europe. Of their curriculum little need be said: it did not differ markedly from that of girls of their age in a thousand schools. Princess Elizabeth was still having regular lessons in music, dancing and drawing. She showed easy competence in them all, but no outstanding genius in any. She had systematic instruction in the Bible; she learned Latin and French, laying the foundation for what has since become a fluent command of the latter language; but she failed to make much headway with German, and after a time gave up the attempt. Mathematics, as has been said, were distinctly not her métier, but geography and history, with a good deal of English literature, became steadily more important in her routine. As childhood drew towards its end she was revealing herself as quick to learn and tenacious to remember, careful and orderly in all her habits of thought; but her mind was of the receptive rather than the creative cast. This was no bad equipment for a twentieth-century Queen, whose function is to draw to herself the characteristic ideas of her people and interpret her subjects to one another, rather than to communicate an originating impulse of her own.

The outbreak of war found the princesses sharing the holiday of the Royal Family at Balmoral, and for a time they remained at Birkhall, on the estate there, in preference to returning to London and becoming involved in the complicated movement for the dispersal of children from the capital. Sandringham was closed as a royal residence for the duration of the war. At the beginning of 1940 they were brought south to Royal Lodge in Windsor Great Park, which had been the country home of the Duke and Duchess of York, and in May they moved into Windsor Castle. They arrived there almost simultaneously with the German invasion of Belgium, and as the *blitzkrieg* developed, with the evacuation of Dunkirk, the downfall of France, the battle of Britain and the imminent threat of a German invasion of England, the question soon arose whether, to secure the future of the dynasty, the heiress ought not to be removed oversea to the hospitable Dominion of Canada. Thousands of less important children were thus being sent into safety, with strong official encouragement; and no one could overlook the possibility that the King might at any moment be killed by German bombs or—a constitutionally more embarrassing fate—taken prisoner by an invading army or a squadron of airborne raiders.

It was scarcely a matter on which Ministers might presume to advise: the choice was necessarily personal to the King and Queen, and they decided with little hesitation that the relief from anxiety offered to other parents was not for them. It was

more important to fortify national morale, as it would be forti-
fied if Princess Elizabeth, representative of her whole generation
of children, remained in the threatened island with those less
fortunate of her generation who could not leave, than to secure
her against the possible physical dangers to come. "The children
won't leave without me," said Queen Elizabeth; "I won't
leave without the King; and the King will never leave."

At the same time there was no point in bringing the princesses
to London to share in the more direct risks the King and Queen
ran, where Buckingham Palace suffered nine direct hits, once
at least with the King and Queen looking out of the window to
see the bomb fall in the quadrangle. They could as yet do nothing
to help, and their business was to get on with their education.
So they remained at Windsor as their normal home for the duration of the war. While squads of soldiers were kept in readiness
to hurry them away from the path of any possible invading army,
they learned the art of bomb disposal with sand buckets and
stirrup-pumps, and practised taking cover in slit trenches dug
in Windsor Great Park.

These might have been years of excitement and danger. As
it turned out, they were years of exceptional seclusion, favour-
able to the quiet business of the schoolroom, though perhaps
less so for the enlargement of human contacts, which is a no less
vital part of the education of a future Queen. At an age when
Princess Elizabeth, in a world at peace, would have been expected to begin her acquaintance with all the most important
people in the land, her circle was narrowly confined, and her
immediate companions limited to the children of a few families
having official positions—some of them quite humble—in and
about the Castle.

She was fourteen when she came to Windsor in the days
before Dunkirk, and it was at this time that Sir Henry Marten,
Provost of Eton College just across the river, was called in to

direct her studies towards subjects necessary for the great position she would one day inherit. Under Sir Henry's supervision, history became the kernel of her work, and especially constitutional history, the study of the growth of the institutional and social order of Great Britain, of the monarchy itself in relation to the Church, Parliament, the Law Courts, the counties, the cities, the universities—all the apparatus of a people's living together in community, of which her father was and she would be the key figure. She was also taken carefully through the outlines of the history of the many nations belonging to the British Commonwealth and Empire, devoting substantial periods of time to the study of colonialism, and the evolution of colonies into sovereign states, and not shrinking from the austere but necessary subject of public finance in peace and war. The study of the past was made to merge into that of contemporary life, and for several years the hours set apart for discussion with the Provost on "Current Affairs" were used to focus the whole of her education on preparation for the tasks awaiting her at an unknown distance in the future.

Already she was marked out as the representative of the generation who were growing up in the course of the war; and she first formally took up that function on October 13, 1940, when she broadcast in the Children's Hour to all the children of the Empire, but with a special message for those whom war had scattered from their homes. "We children at home," she said, "are full of cheerfulness and courage. We are trying to do all we can to help our gallant sailors, soldiers, and airmen, and we are trying, too, to bear our own share of the danger and sadness of war. We know, every one of us, that in the end all will be well." The broadcast was heard in South Africa by the eminent writer, Sarah Gertrude Millin, who wrote in her diary "it was perfectly done. If there are still queens in the world a generation hence, this child will be a good queen".

In speaking for all her contemporaries as wishing for a share

23

in the war effort, the Princess had already enrolled herself for such activity as was possible for a fourteen-year-old girl by putting on the uniform of a Sea Ranger in the Girl Guides. She qualified by the ordinary tests to become bosun of a crew formed among the daughters of the Buckingham Palace staff; and when she reached the age of sixteen and, like everybody else, had to register at the Labour Exchange, she entered this as her form of pre-service training. Two years later, according to the emergency Acts applying to all subjects, she became liable to be directed into full-time employment in some form of war service.

Her eighteenth birthday, a crucial date for all young people in wartime, had an exceptional significance for the Princess. It is commonly stated that the children of the Sovereign come of age at eighteen. This is not true in law, although it is on record that the eighteenth birthday of the future Edward VII was treated in the family as an "informal" coming of age. The position under legislation passed at the beginning of King George VI's reign was this: the Sovereign is always technically of age, but if he or she accedes before the age of eighteen, the royal functions are delegated to a Regent, who is the next adult in the line of succession (at the time the Duke of Gloucester). No subject, however exalted, comes of age before twenty-one. There was a further provision in the Regency Act that if the King were disabled, or absent from the realm, he might delegate some or all of his functions to five joint Councillors of State, who must be the Queen and the next four persons in the line of succession who were of full age.

The effect of this legislation on Princess Elizabeth, after her eighteenth birthday, was that in case of her father's death she would immediately become Queen with the full exercise of her powers; but if he were only temporarily incapacitated she would still be for three years disqualified from discharging the much less onerous functions of a Councillor of State. As her birthday approached, therefore, Parliament at the King's request passed an amending Act to remove this anomaly. It had the effect, not of anticipating her coming of age, but solely of enabling her to act in this one capacity of a Councillor of State. Her services in this office were in fact required almost immediately, when the King sailed in July to visit his forces, including the victors of El Alamein, in the Mediterranean.

Although the Princess attended again and was registered at the Labour Exchange on her eighteenth birthday, the King directed that these new public responsibilities were sufficient, and that she should not be called up. Princess Elizabeth, however, herself demurred. She felt it to be her duty, and indeed she strongly wished, to share as directly as possible in the ordinary wartime experience of girls of her age, and after a tough argument—for both father and daughter inherited a rich measure of the obstinacy that characterizes all the descendants of Queen Victoria—she persuaded the King to change his mind. In March 1945 she was granted an honorary commission as Second Subaltern in the Auxiliary Territorial Service, and was posted to a Mechanical Training Centre at Aldershot. There, suspending for the duration of the course her status as an officer, she was subjected to the full rigour of the N.C.O.'s training in the management and repair of heavy lorries, emerging as a fully qualified driver; but, more important for her future career, she gained experience of living on equal terms under discipline with other young women drawn from the rank and file of the people. She herself probably regretted that this experience was so brief; but the war was now in its last phase; and after she had stood twice, in uniform, on the Palace balcony with her father in the memorable scenes of glory and emotion that celebrated victory over Germany and Japan, there could be no further delay in her devoting herself entirely to the true function of the heir, which is to be at once the deputy and the apprentice of the King.

Already in 1944 she had been given her first lady in waiting,

Lady Mary Strachey, to act as a private secretary and be the nucleus of her personal household. Two more ladies joined her before fighting ended. She had attained a place in the Army List as Colonel of the Grenadier Guards, with which regiment she cultivated the closest possible links. She was inundated with requests to lend her name as president or patron of all manner of good causes, and after taking advice made her selection of the worthiest for acceptance. She became, for example, President of the Queen Elizabeth Hospital for Children at Hackney, of the National Society for the Prevention of Cruelty to Children, of the Cardiff Royal Infirmary, of the Student Nurses' Association; and Patron of the Red Cross Societies of Australia and Canada. She was appointed President, Patron or Vice-Patron of the Royal Albert School, the Life Saving Society, the Royal Navy and Marines' Home at Chatham, the Royal Amateur Orchestral Society, the Welsh Pony and Cob Society; and she was inducted a Bard at the National Eisteddfod of Wales.

These are only a few specimens from a long list. Each appointment was in effect a royal, that is to say public, commendation of the work of the society concerned; and each generally entailed for Princess Elizabeth at least one, and often an annual, visit to the headquarters of the society, the delivery of a speech, the presentation of the staff, and a further enlargement of her contacts with her future subjects.

The Princess was now plainly marked out as the accredited representative of the new post-war generation, the heirs of victory, and she symbolically took up that position by laying her own wreath at the foot of the London Cenotaph in the last armistice celebrations of the old observance, on November 11, 1945. In the following March, she performed her first major public ceremony alone when she sailed to Northern Ireland in the cruiser *Superb*, flying her own banner of arms for the occasion, to launch H.M.S. *Eagle*, then the largest aircraft-carrier afloat, and to deliver a speech in praise of the British shipbuilding industry and the prowess of the Fleet Air Arm in the war. She also attended, on the anniversary of her parents' coronation, the service for the commissioning of H.M.S. *Vanguard*, which she herself had launched in 1944; and it was in this great battleship that she set out, early in the year 1947, with the King, the Queen and Princess Margaret, to make her first acquaintance with the British Commonwealth oversea.

Landing at Duncan Dock, Cape Town, on February 17, 1947, Princess Elizabeth was moving into a new kind of public life. For the first time she was in the presence of a people who had not watched her grow up from childhood, but knew her only as already an adult person in her own right. Her part in the tour was in the main passive: she and her sister walked silently behind or sat quietly beside the King and Queen at innumerable ceremonies in great cities and small townships throughout the four provinces of the Union, while formal speeches were delivered by mayors or native chiefs made their obeisance. They attended banquets, receptions and garden parties, and made such polite conversation as they might with political and civic dignitaries many years their seniors. They carried through a similar routine in the three High Commission Territories of Basutoland, Swaziland and Bechuanaland, and in the two Rhodesias, which have since been amalgamated with Nyasaland in the Central African Federation. Princess Elizabeth's voice was only twice uplifted in public; Princess Margaret's never.

But all the time the heiress to the Throne was making the appeal of youth and grace to the hearts of the diverse races of that divided land; and all the time she herself was enlarging her experience of men and manners against the needs of the years to come. She saw all the physical marvels of the country— Table Mountain, the Drakensberg, the Zambesi, the Victoria Falls—the architectural splendours like Sir Herbert Baker's famous range of government buildings at Pretoria; she saw herds of ostriches and elephants, with an occasional lion in the Kruger National Park; and she was thrown frequently into the society of the veteran soldier and statesman, Field Marshal Smuts, then Prime Minister, who out of the rich store of his memories could vastly enlarge her conception of the family of nations into which she had been born.

Two days of the tour were the Princess's own. On one she performed the opening ceremony of the new graving dock at East London, in the Cape Province, to which her own name was given. The other was her twenty-first birthday and coming of age. On this occasion Smuts himself attended her as she inspected a great parade of the South African Army and took its salute; and, before dividing her evening between two balls given in her honour, in the Town Hall and Government House, she broadcast a birthday message to all the peoples of her father's Empire. In this deeply pondered address she called upon all the boys and girls of her own generation, whose childhood had been lived in the shadows of world war, and who were now coming to maturity, to claim their share of responsibility for the world of peace, and join her in self-dedication to the service of the Commonwealth. Quoting Rupert Brooke's "Now God be thanked Who has matched us with His hour", she asserted for the first time her birthright of leadership and representation of the young, and struck a new note of confidence in the Empire's future.

On her return from South Africa rumours that had been circulating before the tour were speedily confirmed, and in July her engagement was announced to Mr. Philip Mountbatten, Lieutenant in the Royal Navy, who had recently been naturalized under that name after renouncing his foreign titles as a Prince of Greece and Denmark. In the interval before the marriage Princess Elizabeth, now a great public personage, was quietly taking over from the Duke of Gloucester the functions of the chief understudy for the King, both on ceremonial occasions and in maintaining personal contacts with the people. On the King's birthday she had ridden with the King at Trooping the Colour in the traditional position of the Prince of Wales; and the same day he bestowed upon her the Imperial Order of the Crown of India, as a sign of graceful leave-taking between the monarchy and the Indian Empire, which was to become a republic within the Commonwealth a few weeks later. In the intervals between her formal duties the Princess began to study the industrial life of England, visiting factories and workshops in many parts of the country in order to see and talk to her future subjects in the conditions of their daily work.

On November 20, 1947, the King raised Philip Mountbatten to the peerage as His Royal Highness the Duke of Edinburgh, dubbed him knight in the Order of the Garter, and attended his marriage to Princess Elizabeth in Westminster Abbey, the Archbishop of Canterbury solemnizing the rite. The occasion was widely taken as a symbolic emergence of the nation from the austerity of war, and the return of the Household Cavalry to the full magnificence of their peacetime uniforms in order to escort the bride was the outward and visible sign of the mood of rejoicing and relaxation. After a honeymoon divided between the New Forest and Scotland, the Duke and Duchess of Edinburgh took a short lease of a modest country house at Windlesham Moor, near Sunningdale, and spent most of their leisure in fitting out Clarence House, adjoining St. James's Palace, which was to be their residence in London. Their leisure was not unlimited, for the Duke had returned to duty at the Admiralty, and the Princess resigned herself, in her own words, to "being a naval wife". At the sixth centenary celebrations of the Order of the Garter, on St. George's Day, 1948, the most splendid pageant performed in England since the coronation of King George VI, they were solemnly inducted into their stalls as Knight and Lady of the fellowship.

They discharged their first diplomatic mission on behalf of their country at Whitsun that year, when they accepted the invitation of the President of the French Republic to pay a state visit to Paris. After all the agonies and estrangements of the war, the immense acclamation with which the French people received them was readily interpreted as a national renewal of the *Entente Cordiale*.

On November 14, 1948, the first child of Princess Elizabeth was born at Buckingham Palace and given the name Charles Philip Arthur George. The King had already directed that all children of the heiress presumptive should have from birth the title of Prince and the style of Royal Highness, normally bestowed on the Sovereign's grandchildren in the male line only. Soon after the birth the Princess established her home and nursery in Clarence House, and there resumed the routine of royal duties, while the Duke was posted to the Mediterranean Fleet, with headquarters in Malta, where the Princess joined him on an occasional holiday. On August 15, 1950, the anniversary of the end of the Second World War, their daughter Anne Elizabeth Alice Louise was born at Clarence House.

Next year saw the opening of the Festival of Britain, in centenary commemoration of the Great Exhibition of 1851. It was designed as an occasion of national pride and rejoicing; but it was also the year when the anxiety for the health of the King, partly allayed since his dangerous illness of 1948, revived in more ominous form. The Princess was at her father's side when he attended the dedicatory service of the festival in St. Paul's in May; but next month she had to take his place as hostess to King Haakon of Norway and read the King's speech proposing the health of the guest; and a few days later, dressed for the first time in the scarlet uniform of the Brigade of Guards, she rode as deputy for the King and took the salute at Trooping the Colour.

She had been invited by the Canadian Government to spend the autumn, with her husband, in the Dominion; and, although the plan was rather for a holiday visit than a formal tour, elaborate plans had been laid for bringing the Heiress Presumptive into contact with all sorts and conditions of the Canadian people. Almost on the eve of her departure it had to be postponed, for the affliction in the King's leg had recurred and a severe operation had to be performed immediately. For some days the King's life hung in the balance; and when the Princess and the Duke set out, at his urgent desire, directly the immediate danger was passed, both father and daughter were aware that his life was unlikely to be prolonged for more than two years, and might end suddenly at any time.

Travelling by air instead of by sea as originally arranged, in order to catch up with the timetable of the tour, the Princess left England on October 8 with the sense that fate had changed the inner character of the visit. She knew, though the mass of the people of Canada could not, that she was taking a survey of a great nation of which she would in measurable time be the head. The intended informality was not completely preserved, in the face of the determination of the great cities to do honour to their Sovereign's daughter. She had many speeches to make— some of them wholly or partly in French, in compliment to the people of the province of Quebec—and a long and exhausting journey to take right across the vast extent of the Dominion from the Atlantic to the Pacific coast.

In face of the overwhelming reception given to the royal couple all the way along the line, which was probably more demonstrative than anything in her experience hitherto, she showed at first some traces of the shyness she had inherited from her father; but with the unobtrusive but firm support of her husband she gradually overcame her initial diffidence, so much that at the end of the tour a Canadian observer was able to say "We are sending you back a new Princess". Nothing perhaps had made a greater contribution to her education for queenship than this first major imperial mission undertaken in

her own right. In the course of it, moreover, she had been able
to spend two crowded days in the United States, make personal
acquaintance with President Truman, and discover from the
greeting of the American crowds that no people can derive
more passionate excitement from the contemplation of royal
personages than those who are constitutionally vowed to
repudiate the monarchical idea.

Great experience as it had been, however, the Canadian visit
was designed to be no more than a prelude. Year after year since
1948 the King's purpose to sail right round the globe and show
himself to his subjects in East Africa, Ceylon, Australia, New
Zealand and many smaller communities of his Empire had been
frustrated by his frail health. Now at last he had abandoned the
project for himself, but, rather than disappoint the peoples of
the Commonwealth, had decided to send his daughter in his
place. This was to be a tour in greater state than that in Canada,
including such great solemnities as the opening of Parliaments
in the King's name, and elaborate preparations were made and
speeches drafted for many high occasions.

The Royal Family kept Christmas together at Sandringham,
and in mid-January the King and his daughter took leave of one
another at London Airport. It was a poignant leave-taking; for
she was to travel far, to regions whence she could not be recalled in emergency so quickly as she might have been from
Canada, and both were conscious that the parting might easily
be for ever. It was part of the duty that royalty owes to its
subjects that such sorrows must be faced. It turned out as had
been feared. The Princess and her husband had scarcely completed the first stage of their journey, and entered into occupation of the house that had been their wedding present from the
people of Kenya, when news reached them that King George VI
had died quietly in his sleep in the early morning of February 6.
When she descended from her aircraft at London Airport
next day, to be received by Sir Winston Churchill and a line

of Ministers in deep mourning, the Heralds had already proclaimed from the balcony of St. James's Palace the accession
of the Most High and Mighty Princess, Queen Elizabeth the
Second. She was twenty-five years old, as the other Queen
Elizabeth had been at the beginning of her reign. Her life's
work, for which all that had gone before was preparation, had
begun, and from it there would be no withdrawal in this world.

The argument of the next chapter of this study is that the
importance of the Queen in the life of her many peoples resides
not at all in what she does, but entirely in what she is. She
is the embodiment of their tradition and their future, the focus
of their aspiration, the symbol of their unity, their universal
representative. But, because of all that she is, there is a multitude
of things that she must do. It is the purpose of later chapters
to show how the nature of the office that history has imposed
upon her finds expression in her actions and in the disposal of
her crowded days.

The Representative Monarchy

The Representative Monarchy

According to the most conventional description, both by our own textbook-writers and by outside observers, constitutional monarchy is the British system of government. Unfriendly critics are inclined to add that it is an antiquated survival, politically meaningless and out of touch, if not inconsistent, with the spirit of the age—the so-called century of the common man.

If the conventional description came near to being a complete definition, the hostile criticism would be justified. But in fact those who are satisfied with the definition understand only a part, and by no means the most important part, of the British monarchy of 1958. In its deeper meaning for the British peoples it is scarcely a system of government at all. It is their way of life. As such it is necessarily popular; it is always changing and always the same; and it is always up to date.

The conception of monarchy as a way of life is not easy to explain to those who are unaccustomed to it. It can only be fully comprehended from within. To peoples whose social system and patriotic tradition are founded upon revolt against a distant or an authoritarian king—to the Americans and the French, for example—it is apt to seem a paradox. Such as these are inclined to suppose that the British people only continue to tolerate their ancient monarchy because its real content has been emptied out of it by the march of political progress. But it is in truth these foreign critics, themselves cut off by their history from the sources of understanding, who have misconceived the timeless character of monarchy as it has been preserved in the British Commonwealth, and confused the substance with the temporary accidents. In progressively surrendering nearly the whole of its political authority it has not, as they suppose, reduced itself to a shadow of its past greatness: it has refreshed its strength from the original source of its being.

The image of monarchy against which the nations of republican tradition have reacted was mainly shaped during the European Renaissance, when everywhere there was an intense concentration of power in the hands of one man—a Henry VIII or a Philip II or a Louis XIV. It was no doubt natural that when the aspect of "the Prince" most evident to ordinary men was his power over his subjects, to protect or to destroy, this power should be mistaken for the essence of monarchy itself. When and where its arrogance became intolerable the monarchy was destroyed as a thing in which the evil of arbitrary rule was inherent, and a new way of life, the republican way, began its course. Nothing in the following pages is intended to dispute the thesis that the republican way can provide a sound basis for the good life, and the best basis for those peoples whose history and heredity have conditioned them to live by its code. But their success in the modern world does not alter the fact that the thing against which they originally revolted was a phase in the development of monarchy and not its permanent nature.

It is the peculiar happiness of the British peoples that they have survived this phase of the excessive concentration of power in one man's hands: that they have removed the adventitious excrescence and preserved the monarchy—the monarchy itself, not a simulacrum of monarchy. Elizabeth II is just as fully a Queen as ever was Elizabeth I, though without a tithe of her predecessor's personal authority. She is Queen not because she governs England but because England would not be itself without her. The peoples of the United Kingdom have made their brief experiment with the republican way of life and discovered that it was not for them. Mr. Geoffrey Dennis[1] has written of Oliver

---

[1] *Coronation Commentary* (1937), p. 105. It is fair to add that Mr. Dennis has written in the same chapter (p. 80): "Whoso has not once felt the thrill of the word Republic has not loved liberty enough."

Cromwell: "He destroyed the King of England, who soon rose from the dead and was stronger. He destroyed the republic of England without hope or desire of resurrection." The people took back their monarchy and went on moulding it, as they had moulded it for centuries, in the likeness of their changing selves; they are moulding it still.

As we journey away from the social order of the Renaissance despots into an age of ever greater diffusion of power, we begin to see in a clearer perspective the lasting nature of this institution on which the excrescence of arbitrary authority was for a time deposited. We perceive that it has come into existence and been preserved through the ages in response to some innate need of the human heart—and Man, whatever Aristotle may say, is something more than a political animal. The thing we have to study is nothing less than human nature itself; but in the present century the archaeologists and anthropologists have done much to help us. Peering into the depths of prehistory they have made it clear that kingship does not begin as a political device.

The earliest discernible King is not a warlord or a lawgiver, but a figure of sacred or magical significance. In one sense he embodies in his person the life of the tribe; in another the dimly apprehended forces that enable them to live. Remotely in the mysterious relics of palaeolithic hunters we seem to see the ritual figure of a dedicated man who impersonated the animal that is their quarry and so secured its fertility; more clearly, as neolithic man learns the arts of agriculture, we can see in innumerable examples how the magical King is identified with the life of the crops or with the sunshine and rain by which their growth is assured. With his health the tribe prospers; his sickness may entail the failure of the harvest; his death is only prevented from symbolizing tribal disaster because in a profounder sense it can be identified with the falling of the seed into the ground, as prelude to the universal springtime resurrection, of which his successor will be the incarnation.

39

These ideas, which are visibly alive in the belief and practice of many of the less advanced races of the contemporary world, are also traceable in the remote past of every European people. In the conscious mind they are inevitably superseded as progress disentangles magic from science and metaphor from thought, and as superstition gives way to a profounder sense of spiritual values. But their world-wide prevalence and incalculably long survival testify that they respond to a universal need of human nature, which must still be satisfied though the ideas by which it was once met have been found insufficient. The British Commonwealth satisfies that need by placing at the apex of its society a single personality who is felt to be the universal representative. How real is that sense of representation to-day was shown by the profound emotions that swept the people at the time of the present Queen's coronation five years ago. As the great and solemn rites took their stately course, and for the first time were made visible to the multitudes by the new miracle of television, the whole nation felt itself to be rededicated in the person of the Queen. Of the millions throughout the world-wide Commonwealth who were exalted by that great uplifting of the heart, there were probably few to reflect that they were repeating the experience of their earliest Christian ancestors; but there is evidence that, in the centuries when the pagan tribes who had swept over the Roman Empire were being converted to the Christian faith, it was usual for the King to be baptized on behalf of all his people, and that out of that mystical representation the later ritual of coronation arose.[1]

Now most nations have a representative personality at their head. He may be the effective director of the daily business of government, as in the United States; he may be, as in France, a distinguished elder statesman who intervenes only occasionally,

[1] See especially *Le Roi Très Chrétien*, by Comte Jean de Pange (Paris, 1949).

when the machine of government is in danger of breaking down.[1] But in nearly all republics the President is or has lately been a politician, and his representation is overwhelmingly political and therefore incomplete. The Queen of England represents universally. She is the embodiment of the whole life of the people: she presides indeed over its political action, but only because politics are one of the necessary departments of life, and of all departments she is the head.

Her relation to political power, which is the slow growth of many centuries, has to-day the subtlety characteristic of very ancient things. In any personal sense there are many authorities in the state who are much more powerful than she. Informally, since she remains in her place while parties and their leaders come and go, she may in time come to exercise by her accumulating experience an influence upon the minds of her ministers which far transcends those theoretical powers which in fact she never uses—for when her ministers tender their formal "advice" she is bound by the Constitution to follow it. Such an influence became very real in the hands of her grandfather, King George V; it did not rise so high in her father's time, merely because of his shorter reign. For the Queen herself, who as yet has experience only of one party in office, it is in the main an endowment that the future will bestow. But though she may be expected to outlive every politician now serving in her Cabinets or her Parliaments, the contribution that she can then make by virtue of a long memory to political wisdom will not be the fundamental aspect of her relation to government, which depends not upon what she says or does but upon what she is. Her essential function is less to exercise power than to keep power in its proper proportion to the totality of life.

It is a British characteristic to regard the worship of power as extremely vulgar. So the real possessors of power have to wield

[1] Written while the new, Gaullist, constitution for the French Republic remains in draft.

it under the eye of someone who is not herself powerful, but yet has to be treated with the utmost deference. The rulers of the state are called her Ministers, that is, her servants; and by the ceremonial behaviour demanded of them in her presence they are reminded at every turn that their authority is a form of service. That which they serve is the people, made visible in the Queen; but since her representation extends over such a much wider field than that in which their service is rendered, the essential lesson they are taught is that power has to be subordinate to a larger conception of life. The Queen, who is less powerful than they, is nevertheless more important; she has a stronger hold on the imagination of the people over whom, in her name, they are set. Every time a commander-in-chief stands to attention and salutes her, or a Prime Minister presents his humble duty and begs leave to explain the policy his Government—her Government, rather—intends to pursue, he is reminded afresh that authority has to be exercised with humility. This is the great British security against any danger that a successful soldier or a popular statesman may begin to mistake himself for the source of his own authority, and so fall into the habit of thought by which dictators are made.

Of every major department of the nation's life the Queen is the head; and thus she is the symbol of the nation's unity. All the armed forces serve under her commission and fight in her name. She is the supreme Governor of the established Church of England. She is the source of justice; the leading practitioners of the law are dignified with the title of Queen's Counsel; and wrongdoing is punished, not as a transgression of any private interest, but as a breach of the Queen's peace. She confirms in office the greater local officials—herself, for example, "pricking" the names of the sheriffs for the year, who are to be the social heads of their counties as she is the social head of the nation; she asserts the nation's respect for learning by giving to eminent scholars the rank of Regius

Professor; gives the title "Royal" to the Academy in which the nation's most representative artists are associated and to the Society that incorporates the leaders in the world of natural science; extends her patronage to innumerable bodies devoted to the encouragement of charity, healing, education, industry or sport. She is called the Fountain of Honour: decorations and titular rewards for all kinds of public service are personally conferred by her. Her representative name inscribed at the head of the roll in all honourable branches of national activity is the assurance that sailors, soldiers and airmen, lawyers, scholars, scientists and workers in industry are members of a single service, and that service directed to the enrichment of the life of a united people.

In all that she touches the Queen represents the whole in relation to the part. Where she lends her name to any specialist activity, she intimates symbolically that the entire community takes an interest in it. But the Queen is much more than a symbol: she stands peculiarly for the idea that the ultimate reality in corporate life—at the heart of what sometimes seems the chilly and soulless machinery of the modern state—is not an abstraction, but a human being of like passions with ourselves. Because she is not a symbol but a person she can, as she moves about her dominions, bring the representation of the whole into direct contact with every part. Wherever she goes, that spot is momentarily the centre of the Commonwealth, and the soldier on parade, the artisan at his bench, the nurse by the bedside and the patient under her care are enabled to feel themselves exalted by the recognition of their place in a worldwide family and a vast design.

The nation and Commonwealth expect their Sovereign to be above all a mirror of the normal member of their close-knit community, the ordinary young woman, idealized perhaps, but raised to outstanding stature only by the extraordinary position to which she has been called. Her grandfather, George V, never tired of describing himself as an ordinary man, and brought up his children and grandchildren in the same model. He created a picture in the eyes of his English subjects of their King as the most English of them all, the type that any average man believing in the British way of life would wish to be, if he could breathe the spacious air that is the environment of royalty. But if the Queen is to be the embodiment of ordinary English life, she must be seen living in ordinary human relationships. Therefore the Royal Family is as indispensable to the representative work of queenship as the Queen herself.

The private lives of herself, her husband and children, her mother and sister are—as part of their service—lived to a very large degree in public. Their concerns are followed with the most intense and sometimes embarrassing popular interest, which extends to the amusements they indulge in, the food they eat and the clothes they wear. Trivial or crude as are some manifestations of this interest, they proceed from the healthy fact that the people have before their eyes a picture not of an ideal woman but of an ideal group, so that families in mansion or cottage may be strengthened in their inward relationships by the feeling—it scarcely amounts to a thought— that the little social unit they are maintaining is one that also lives and develops in its most admirable form in Windsor Castle or Buckingham Palace.

After the Queen herself, the most important member of this group is of course her Consort, the Duke of Edinburgh. He has practically no official powers or functions. Supposing that the Queen were absent from England while he remained at home, he would be one of the five members of the Royal Family to whom, under the title of Councillors of State, most of her formal duties would be delegated; but since he normally and naturally accompanies the Queen in her travels, such occasions are likely to be rare. None has yet occurred. He is

not crowned, and none of the mystical aura of monarchy sur-
rounds him. He has no share in the Queen's daily intercourse
with her ministers of state, and, though he is a member of the
House of Lords, convention requires that he take no part of
his own in party politics, lest the impartiality of the Throne be
compromised. Officially, then, he is scarcely known to the
Constitution. But his is perhaps the most influential *unofficial*
voice in the land. Because he is the Queen's husband, everybody
listens to him with loyal attention; and because he is himself,
a young man with a mind of his own, and a vigorous and provoca-
tive enthusiasm for all that is energetic, progressive and masculine in the nation's life and work, especially in industry,
technology and sport, he has become a constant stimulus to all
that is most vital, especially among the young. Any picture of
the representative monarchy at work must find a place in the
foreground for his activity.

Because the Queen came to her position by birth and not
by any contest, there is among her subjects no section of
qualified or reluctant loyalty who voted against her appointment,
no defeated candidate looking forward to another opportunity
to supplant her. She is able to maintain equally friendly personal
relations with all parties in the state, any of which may in turn
provide her with a government. Though the Constitution
requires her to talk politics only with those who for the time
being possess the confidence of the people, as expressed through
the House of Commons, there is no such limit on her social
contacts; and leaders of all parties are accustomed to meet
in her house as her friends, and therefore as friends of one
another. This tradition of personal good-will between political
opponents is strongly rooted in the British tradition, and is
displayed in the social life of Parliament as well as in that of the
royal circle. But it is to be remembered that Parliament itself
meets in a Royal Palace at the invitation of the Queen; and
there is much profound symbolism in the custom that, when

she takes her place on the Throne at the state opening and summons the Commons to attend her, the Prime Minister and the Leader of the Opposition walk together to the House of Lords, having suspended all their differences in the presence of their hostess.

It is also by virtue of her hereditary position that the Queen is able to symbolize the continuity of the national tradition across the centuries. For she is linked by blood with her predecessors in whose names the ancient glories were won, and with her successors on whom the hopes of the future are fixed. In this as in so much else the institution of monarchy corresponds to the natural instincts of the ordinary man whose idealized representative it is: for he does not wish, when his time comes, to hand on his place in society to a stranger selected by some plebiscitary process as best equipped to fill it, but to the issue of his own blood. It is the royal family, a continuous line of human beings running through the ages, that stands simultaneously for the unity of the people at each separate point of time and for the continuity of its life through all time's changes.

The Queen is also the symbol of unity across the separations of space. As the many dependencies of the British Empire come one by one to maturity, they are released from any political control by the Government and Parliament at Westminster; but most of them have freely decided to remain members of the Commonwealth of which the Queen is the head. Three members in Asia have chosen to become republics; they regard the Queen as external to their national life, although they recognize her presidency of the Commonwealth of Nations in which they are content to retain an equal partnership. This difference of attitude to the monarchy is to be accepted without repining as a fair statement, in terms of the metaphor in which the social order of the Commonwealth is habitually expressed, of a fundamental difference of social philosophy. In each of the kingdoms that are governed in her name, the Queen stands as the symbol and pattern of a way of life that was first developed in the British Isles and has been transported or copied oversea. Republican India, Pakistan and Ceylon, by denying to the Queen a place within their national structure, have with perfect propriety indicated that the British way of life is not their way, and that they do not choose to assimilate themselves to it. Each of them is the home of an ancient and complex civilization; they are faithful to the profound faiths and creeds of their ancestors, which are not the Christianity in which the British monarchy is rooted; they will continue to build their social order on the foundations they know. It follows that, while they are wholehearted in their adherence to the Commonwealth, their association with the other partners, and with one another, is less intimate than that of membership in one family: it is limited to the domain of the political and diplomatic co-operation of the Commonwealth. To them the Queen is a political, not a universal, representative. It is not therefore surprising that, although the Queen has repeatedly expressed her desire to extend her direct acquaintance with all the nations of her Commonwealth, and has in fact travelled, before or since her accession, in all its independent kingdoms except the two newest, Ghana and Malaya, she has yet to pay her first visit to the less intimately associated communities of India and Pakistan. Her relationship there is to the governments and not directly to the peoples, so that it is less important that the people should know her personally and by her be known.

At the date when these pages are written, Malaya has not yet completed six months of independence, and it would be rash to attempt to forecast what its permanent relationship to the monarchy will be. One of its own princes has been set up as head of the State under the suzerainty of the Queen, and it would seem likely that, if a symbol for the national way of life is felt to be required, the instincts of the people will attach themselves most readily to their native dynasties. On the other hand, it is a land where an immigrant race of distinct culture, the Chinese, are as numerous as the native-born Malays themselves; and if the two are to coalesce into a single nation, the symbol of a Sovereign far away, belonging to neither by blood and therefore having equal care for both, may yet have its unifying value. While these ambiguities remain unresolved, nothing more will be said here of the place and function of the Queen in Malaya—which she has not yet visited, although other members of the Royal Family have done so on her behalf.

In Africa, in contrast to Asia, the British Empire into which so much of the continent was absorbed in the nineteenth century brought contact with an admittedly higher civilization than any that was native to the soil. Advancement in civilization was therefore synonymous with the adoption of an increasing measure of the British way of life, including generally the Christian religion which is the source of its ideals. That is to say, the African communities, whether under tutelage or after their promotion to independent status, have aspired to take the colour of British civilization even while working to release themselves from British political control. Their tendency is to become, so to speak, agnatic members of the family of which the Queen is the head, and they can without difficulty receive her as the symbol of their internal cohesion (which is not in all cases naturally easy to maintain), as well as of their association with the Commonwealth. For Ghana, then, as well as for Canada, Australia, New Zealand, South Africa, the Federation of Rhodesia and Nyasaland, and several colonies now on the brink of independent sovereignty, the Queen is not only the Head of the Commonwealth but the head of each member separately. It is only in a narrowly theoretical sense that she is their supreme governor. But they may all look to her, in her many unpolitical aspects, as universal and supreme representative; and in her travels among them, which become ever more frequent, she is welcomed everywhere as the head of the local family. (She is the first reigning Sovereign of any nationality to circumnavigate the globe; and in doing so she scarcely set foot outside her own territory.) To each independent nation, and indeed to each dependent colony, she can be and is a symbol of unity, of the ideas common to all of the British allegiance concerning justice, tolerance, liberty, the love of peace, the fundamental decencies of family life.

All civilized peoples love these things; nevertheless there is a distinctive attitude to each of them which has grown up within the British family of nations and been formed by its history; and the assurance that the identity of conception shall not dissolve away as these nations become politically distinct is the fact that they can all continue to see their ideals symbolized in the person of the same Queen.

It follows from this conception of representative monarchy that the meaning of the royal office in kingdom and Common-wealth resides not in what the Queen does but in what she is. If she had come to the Throne in infancy and a Regent had been required by law; if in old age she found it necessary to delegate most of her formal functions to her son, the Prince of Wales, she and not her deputy would still be the focus of her peoples' hopes. But because of what she is, because she has to answer the challenge to represent in action the ideals and aspirations of so many and diverse peoples, a life of unremitting public service is required of her. It is the purpose of the following chapters to describe how her busy hours are and have been spent.

The Daily Round

The Daily Round

A LATER chapter will be devoted to the Queen's work in what is now called "public relations"—that is to say, going out among her people, pursuing their acquaintance, and, in making herself known to them, helping them to know themselves and one another, because the Queen represents all, and whenever she visits any localized community she is opening windows for them upon a larger world. Each of these visits, however, removes her, not from the centre of the national life, for she is herself the centre and momentarily confers central importance upon every place she visits, but from her own geographical headquarters at Buckingham Palace. Each visit has to be contrived, usually many months beforehand, so as not to derange the very detailed and exacting routine of her headquarters functions. The present chapter will look at that routine, and see how the Queen's day is actually spent when her presence at some more distant function is not required, or cannot be granted.

The framework of routine is the Queen's family life, which hinges upon the nurseries on the top floor of Buckingham Palace, looking out over the Queen Victoria Memorial and the Mall. Whenever she is at home she spends three-quarters of an hour with her children—or with Princess Anne when the Prince of Wales is at school—between 8.45 in the morning and 9.30. There is an equally definite period in the evening, from a quarter to five till half-past six, which is kept free for the children if in any way possible; and occasionally their mother lunches with them, but this is rare because of the multitude of official engagements. During the holidays, of course, whether at Windsor, Sandringham or Balmoral, there is much more time to devote to them; probably they are not separated from their parents much more than children of less exalted families in term time—for it has to be remembered that nowadays Princess Anne as well as her brother is busy then. She is doing regular lessons under a governess with two other little girls.

Before the children come down in the morning to her rooms on the first floor of the Palace, the Queen has already break-fasted and done some preparation for the day's work. All the national daily newspapers are supplied to the Palace; they have been surveyed by the private secretaries, who have marked or cut out the columns most likely to be of interest and importance to the Queen. The Queen studies predominantly news rather than views—she has any amount of opinion supplied to her by word of mouth by the eminent people who come for audiences—but important leading articles from the weightier papers are cut out for her and preserved for reference. When Parliament is sitting she has also before her the report on the previous day's proceedings which it is the duty of the Vice-Chamberlain of the Household—a junior member of the the Government—to write for her at the end of every night's sitting and send by special messenger to the Palace before he goes home. The Queen always reads this report with close attention, and can face an examination on its contents—or conduct one, as has sometimes been discovered by an inexperienced Vice-Chamberlain who supposed himself to be producing no more than a formal state-ment, destined to be consigned unread to the pigeon-hole or the waste-paper basket. The Queen's retentive memory is also applied to what she reads in the newspapers, and she takes a rather mischievous pleasure in catching out her staff on matters relating to the day's news.

All this preparation has been disposed of long before half-past nine, when Princess Anne goes upstairs to begin her lessons and the Queen sits down at her desk to cope with the morning's office work. The Duke of Edinburgh, who has office work of his own of a rather different kind, goes off to his own room at the same time.

The Queen of course receives every day a large personal correspondence, much of it from complete strangers. All kinds of people, some responsible, some eccentric, and many just crazy, write to her on every conceivable subject, generally asking her to intervene with her authority in some cause or project in which they are interested. There are invitations to give her patronage to an infinite variety of public functions, many or most of them for extremely deserving objects, but in far greater number than the time at her disposal for journeys out of London, which is very limited, will allow her to accept. There are petitions for her support or opposition to this, that or the other Bill before Parliament—which of course it would be quite unconstitutional for her to attempt to influence in any way until it comes to her for the Royal Assent; and that, on the advice of her Ministers, she always gives. There are pitiful appeals for mercy from the relations of men in prison or under sentence of death—these last happily less frequent now than before recent legislation restricting the category of capital murder. And among the rest there are a certain number of letters on truly domestic matters that involve no public interest. There is also as a rule a bundle of naïve little compositions, full of loyalty and affection, from children up and down the land.

It is the first daily duty of the private secretaries to sort out this very various correspondence. All are acknowledged, even those from manifest lunatics. Those which in any way concern public affairs or the functions of the Queen as head of the State— and this includes the appeals for mercy—are forwarded to the appropriate government departments: usually the Home Office or the Scottish Office, for it is the Secretaries of State for these two departments who advise the Queen on the unspecialized relations with her subjects in England and Scotland respectively. But some go to the Foreign Office or the Commonwealth Relations Office; for the post comes from all over the world. The letters from children are passed to one of the ladies-in-waiting, who are thought to have a more sympathetic touch than the male staff, and a quicker insight into the nursery point of view. Those letters which can be readily classified under headings of pure routine, for which there are standing instructions, are answered in a common form by the private secretaries. Those which are a little less stereotyped are taken upstairs and shown to the Queen herself, who gives her directions as to how they shall be answered. Finally, the Queen will select some that are genuinely personal, which she will wish to answer with her own hand. This is normally the smallest group, but it is larger than many people suppose; for the Queen is a conscientious correspondent, and likes if in any way possible to answer herself letters that are at all personal and come from writers whom she knows even slightly.

For example, if a personal reminiscence may be forgiven, I addressed a letter of condolence to the new Queen on the day of the death of King George VI. I had had only occasional and very humble contact with her as princess, I held no official position of any kind, and my letter must have been one of thousands, most of them from people of much greater importance. I expected nothing but a formal acknowledgment from a private secretary, or perhaps merely a printed card. I was surprised and touched to receive a two-page reply hand-written by the Queen, in a style of absolute informality and simplicity. These personal letters are initialled by Her Majesty "E.R." in the corner of the envelope and come either by messenger from the Palace or by registered post—no doubt because the Queen's handwriting in the address, if recognized, would present an obvious temptation to the acquisitive through whose hands they might pass.

After the letters that have come by the post the Queen has to grapple with the documents that have been brought by messengers from No. 10 Downing Street and the departments in Whitehall. This is the routine that appears in the diaries of King George V as "doing my boxes"; for communications from members of the Government are sent to the Queen in red-leather-covered dispatch boxes, each with a lock to which the Queen has one key and the Minister the other. All the year round there is never any respite from the "boxes"; for though Parliament may go into recess the work of the departments goes on. They do not cease even when the Queen is on holiday; the daily boxes arrive by train at Windsor, Sandringham or Balmoral, and even in the slackest season the Queen cannot expect to dispose of them in less than three-quarters of an hour. The only exception is on Monday; for with the advance of the modern week-end, although the departments do a half-day's work on Saturday, the Minister is generally in his constituency and is nowadays unlikely to be sending off anything for the Queen's approval until Monday morning, unless a real emergency is in sight.

The contents of the boxes are partly for the Queen's approval, partly for her information. Under the latter heading she receives a sufficient selection of the telegrams sent to the Foreign Office in the last twenty-four hours to keep her informed of the state of British relations with Powers all round the world, and give her the inside story of the happenings of which she has already read the outline in the morning newspapers. It is necessary to skim for her the cream of these telegrams, for there are sixty or seventy embassies and legations all sending confidential reports to London daily, and the total bulk of their communications is enormous.

The Cabinet papers are less voluminous, for in ordinary times it sits only once a week, and the Queen is able to absorb some of the milk as well as the cream. These papers are in some degree a supplement to the daily parliamentary report she gets from the Vice-Chamberlain of the Household; but they contain much that is secret, and that the Vice-Chamberlain could not include in his report even if it were relevant, since he is not a member of the Cabinet. There are in addition many communications from the nations of the Commonwealth oversea. Under the modern constitution of the Statute of Westminster, which makes these nations fully sovereign, their correspondence does not pass through the Commonwealth Relations Office in Whitehall, or any other United Kingdom department of state, but comes to the Queen either direct from their capitals or through the High Commissioners whom they all maintain in London.

The reports have of course all been collated already by the Governor-General of the country concerned, who is the Queen's personal representative and exercises all her functions on the spot; and it is only the resultant distillation that needs to be transmitted to her. Nevertheless the total bulk of information from the Commonwealth is considerable. The republican members in Asia, in whose internal affairs neither the Queen nor any representative of hers has any function, are, if anything, more assiduous than the monarchies in supplying her with confidential intelligence.

All this information is discussed with, and if necessary amplified by, one or more of the private secretaries, who may sometimes be instructed to obtain further explanation from the departments concerned. In that case there may be another session of the same kind in the evening, to consider the replies that have been obtained. But besides information about the state of public affairs, the red boxes will also contain a number of documents that require the Queen's action or consent: in most cases, no doubt, purely formal, but not to be given until the subject-matter of the application has been mastered, for it will probably be necessary for the Queen to show understanding of it when next she meets the Minister whose advice she is accepting or the person affected by the action he wishes to take.

Sometimes she will be asked to sanction a dispatch which it is proposed to send to a foreign government. She cannot, it is true, do anything compulsively if she dislikes it: the Foreign Secretary, so long as he remains in office, is entitled to expect that the Sovereign will be guided by the "advice"—a technical constitutional term—that he formally gives. But the Sovereign for her part is entitled to be fully informed of the nature and implications of the action he is taking in her name; she has, in Bagehot's famous analysis, not only the right to be informed, but the right to be consulted and the right to warn. There is one memorable instance in which Queen Victoria carried the right to warn so far that she asked her Foreign Secretary, Lord Russell, to accept a version of one of his dispatches which she, with the help of the Prince Consort, had entirely rewritten, believing that as originally drafted it would have involved the country in war with the United States. Lord Russell gave way. He was not bound to do so. Had he persisted in his advice the Queen was bound to accept it, on pain of the resignation of her Government with the probable impossibility of forming another. But historians have generally agreed that the Queen saved the situation.

This was nearly a hundred years ago, and the monarchy has travelled far. But the influence Queen Victoria then exerted in the cause of peace could still be exerted today. It has nothing to do with the prerogative powers of the Crown: it depends solely upon the personal right of the Sovereign to be consulted, and as a reserve will grow continually in effectiveness as she herself advances in experience and knowledge of international affairs. It is for this reason that it is vital to maintain the custom that requires the Foreign Secretary to be ready to explain beforehand every important step of policy that he is taking. He will leave the office when his party falls from power; but she will remain, and her accumulated memories will be available to help his successors, perhaps in some dangerous crisis of international affairs.

Apart from such interruptions as these, the ordinary morning's work at Buckingham Palace lies mainly on the borderline between the Queen's general functions as head of society and her special functions as head of the State. The very large correspondence that has come in to the Private Secretary's office in the past twenty-four hours spreads itself indiscriminately over both sides of her activity. Not all of it has come by post; the red boxes brought by civil service messengers from the Government departments in Whitehall account for a substantial part of it. So also do the communications from the High Commissioners of the Commonwealth, through whom come the reports, petitions and other official papers sent by the Governors-General who represent the Queen in her realms oversea.

So far as these deal with political matters the Governor-General is acting as little more than a post office; for the full authority of the Crown in the country where he presides is delegated to him, and what he does in the Queen's name does not, except in the rarest cases, require any further confirmation from her. He acts politically for her on the advice of the Ministers responsible to the Parliament he convenes, exactly as she acts on the advice of the Ministers at Westminster. But it is necessary that she shall know the main lines of what is being done on her behalf; and moreover, there is much that is un-political—requests for royal patronage of some good cause, notifications of the impending visit of some eminent oversea subject to whom some royal courtesy might suitably be extended, perhaps even an invitation for the Queen herself or a member of the royal family to visit the country—to swell the correspondence.

All these letters have to be studied with particular care, for this is one of the ways in which the Queen keeps herself informed of affairs in all the countries over which she reigns. There is no more important function of the modern monarchy: it has to be remembered that there is to-day no other, in England or anywhere else, who has quite the same duty, or quite the same opportunity, to build up a mental picture of the whole unity in diversity of the Commonwealth and Empire. Neither of the Secretaries of State, for Commonwealth Relations and for the Colonies, is concerned with more than a part of the Queen's territories oversea, and moreover both of these are limited to a political view.

Professors of Commonwealth history, economics or law in the universities may indulge themselves with a wider outlook on the life of the peoples; but they lack the special sources of information open to the Queen, from whom no official secrets are withheld. Gifted as she undoubtedly is with a particularly receptive mind and a retentive memory, she will in the course of years acquire an inside knowledge of the entire family of nations which must be in its own way unique.

Thus the Queen, after six years on the Throne, is in process of acquiring a wider knowledge of the affairs of the Commonwealth over which she presides than is obtainable by any other person. Let not this statement be misunderstood. Width is not the same thing as depth. It would of course be absurd to suppose that the Queen can rival her statesmen in understanding the many aspects of any one problem, or any one country, with which they have to deal, and which they have been constantly discussing in their departments, in Cabinet, and in Parliament. She sees only the resultant of it all, when the discussions have been completed and a decision is reported for her assent. She is mentally fed, so to speak, on pre-digested food. What is unique to her is her detachment, and the panoramic view that she is given. She stands at an equal intellectual distance from each realm of the Commonwealth, and from each subject of policy: she can bring them all to a focus, undisturbed by any specialism that might spoil the perspective. This at least is the theory and the ideal.

It is a legitimate criticism of the practice that the Queen spends so much the greater part of her time in the United Kingdom that the perspective in which she views the other nations of the Commonwealth is bound to be somewhat distorted. This distortion, such as it is, is the inevitable legacy of a past age in which London actually was the centre of government for the whole Empire; and as the Commonwealth of sovereign nations continues its development the demand may well arise that the unbalance be corrected by the Queen's distributing her life more evenly among them. Meanwhile the Queen is herself fully aware of the temptation to bias, and takes great pains to guard against it, as the multiplicity of her lines of communication to the Commonwealth oversea equips her to do. In any event, there is no other person whose standpoint is so central; and it is undoubtedly a factor in preserving the unity of the Commonwealth, which has so few formal bonds of association, that there should exist one person specially placed so as to be able to see it as a whole.

Turning now from this survey of the Queen's morning correspondence, it is time to consider some of the routine appointments that continue her working day. One class of these is seldom regarded by the less thoughtful of her critics, but takes up a surprising amount of her time. The Queen, among amateurs, is probably the busiest artist's model in the land. Except in high summer, and sometimes even then, she is always sitting for her portrait, frequently for more than one. There are sixty or seventy British embassies and high commissions distributed round the globe, each of which may reasonably look forward to being decorated with an oil painting of the Queen. So may many official residences of Governors-General and Prime

Ministers; service headquarters, charitable or learned institutions under royal patronage, may have a claim or at least an expectation. Consequently the production of these portraits goes on as a steady industry nearly all the year round, and the Queen on the average is giving six or seven sittings to painters every month. Sometimes she goes herself to the studio to sit; sometimes the artist is invited to stay at Windsor. When there is added the constant demand for fresh photographic portraits— and incidentally the need to give a due share of her patronage to all professional photographers of sufficiently high repute— it will be appreciated that this business of making her features visibly familiar to her subjects is not the least onerous of the Queen's regular labours.

The Government of Queen Elizabeth I issued a very small number of official likenesses of Her Highness, which alone were authorized for publication by the closely supervised printing presses, and had to do duty for years; but the twentieth century, with its passion for the visual publicity of far less important people, would certainly not tolerate any such monotony in the portrayal of the Sovereign.

Apart from such abnormal, but frequent, engagements as these sittings, the morning hours remaining after the disposal of correspondence are usually occupied by a succession of individual interviews. A surprisingly large variety of people come to see the Queen. Some of them come for purposes that are at first sight purely personal; for example the dressmakers, and the jewellers. All women of position devote a good deal of time to the fitting of their clothes; but with the Queen this is not a private indulgence but a public duty. She is perpetually playing a part, and must be suitably costumed for every scene in which she appears.

A considerable variety of dress is expected of her; if she wears for a visit to some provincial town clothes that are already too familiar from the newspapers, the townspeople will

63

be disappointed and the mayor will probably take offence. Everything she wears will be minutely studied and if possible copied by many of her own sex, and rigorously criticized by others; for loyal subjects who would think it the height of bad taste and bad manners to animadvert upon the behaviour of their Sovereign feel no such inhibitions about her wardrobe. Every woman who comes into her presence will have taken immense pains over her toilette for the occasion; and the Queen must not be outshone.

She has to steer a middle course, not compromising her dignity by running after the latest eccentricities of fashion, yet not clinging to the established to the extent of seeming out of date. Consequently, the dress designers who serve her have a delicate responsibility. She has to spend many hours in consultation with them; and they are rewarded by the knowledge that the mere fact of their selection by her gives them authority to influence the whole field of women's fashions.

There is in addition a part of her wardrobe which is not subject to fashion but is prescribed for great official occasions. To this part belong, for example, the crimson velvet Parliament robe, and the stately mantles of the Orders of the Garter and the Thistle, with all their elaborate associated insignia. She is, on the other hand, relieved of a King's necessity to maintain a great variety of service uniforms. That duty she is able to depute to her Consort. The Queen herself wears no uniform except that of the Brigade of Guards; but even so, she has to keep five distinct scarlet tunics, with the buttons and badges adjusted to the patterns of the five regiments of the Brigade. Uniforms and official robes, however, change but rarely, and account for only a small fraction of the time that the Queen has to devote to keeping her wardrobe equipped for all her duties.

When all these various claims on the Queen's time have been allowed for, the main business of the average morning is the reception of individuals, some of great public importance, others of only moderate distinction, but all in some degree representative of some aspect of their country's life. The country for this purpose is by no means always one of those owning the Queen's allegiance. Among the endless stream of diverse visitors that flows day after day through the gilded gates of Buckingham Palace, a very substantial proportion are foreigners. There are about sixty embassies and legations in London; and every new Ambassador or Minister comes to "present his credentials" to the Queen. Every outgoing Ambassador also comes to take formal leave.

When a new Ambassador is to be received one of the vast and ponderous horse-drawn royal coaches is sent by the Crown Equerry to fetch him from his Embassy; he appears in full-dress diplomatic uniform with all his decorations, and accompanied by the senior members of his Embassy staff. The Queen is attended by the Secretary of State for Foreign Affairs, who introduces the Ambassador; the Ambassador then presents the official letters from his Government announcing his appointment, and the letters recalling his predecessor. He then makes formal presentation of the members of his staff, whether they are newcomers or already known to the Queen, for theoretically they are different persons as his subordinates from what they were as subordinates of their previous chief.

Apart from the handing over of the documents, which the Foreign Secretary will eventually deposit in the archives of his department, the formal proceedings do not go beyond a brief exchange of compliments; but unless the programme of the day is exceptionally crowded the Queen will always ask the Ambassador to stay for some more private and informal talk about the affairs of his country, and probably to remain to luncheon, where he, and his wife if he is married, will be able to make the acquaintance of the Duke of Edinburgh as well.

No other of the Queen's morning visitors, not even her own

Cabinet Ministers, require to be received with such elaborate protocol as the Ambassadors of foreign powers. But all British Ambassadors about to depart for their posts have a claim to be received by the Queen, and generally will be received again if they are recalled to London for important consultations at the Foreign Office, and eventually when they vacate office. The same general principle applies to the holders of most other appointments of similar eminence. The Queen has both a right and a duty to be in touch with what is going on in every branch of public life throughout her dominions, and whenever possible draws her information from the fountain head, from the man actually in charge. Thus she receives every new Governor of a colony, and *a fortiori* every Governor-General of a sovereign member of the Commonwealth on his appointment, or immediately on his arrival at his first visit to London, if he is already a resident of the country over which he is to preside. Commanders in Chief in any of the armed services also come. So do Bishops, who, by the curious constitution of the Church of England, as stereotyped under Elizabeth I, are elected by their chapters on receiving a *congé d'élire*, a permission to elect, from the Queen.

The *congé d'élire* is invariably accompanied by letters missive containing the name of the person to be elected; and although the bishop cannot be consecrated until the election has been freely made, the dean and chapter incur the dire pains and penalties of "praemunire" if they elect anyone other than the person named. Thus the Bishops whom the Queen receives on their appointment have in fact though not in theory been actually appointed by her. Her choice, as with secular offices, is made on the advice of the Prime Minister, which she is constitutionally bound to accept, if he presses it.

This, however, is one of the departments of State in which the Prime Minister, who is not bound to be a member of the Church of England, does not always claim particular competence, and if the Queen should develop definite personal leanings in relation to it, she might not improbably induce him to modify his advice to suit her wishes, in a way that his parliamentary responsibilities would not permit him to do on an issue of secular politics. Certainly Queen Victoria concerned herself deeply with the higher Church appointments, and exercised heavy pressure on her Ministers in settling them, generally after consulting clerical friends of her own, of whom Dr. Randall Davidson, afterwards Archbishop of Canterbury, was for long the most intimate.

The point is at the moment theoretical: the present Queen, though a devout daughter of the Church of England, has so far shown no definite predilections in ecclesiastical politics. But this is one of the departments of government in the broad sense—her title in the Church of England is "Supreme Governor"—in which the constitutional control of the royal prerogative is least clearly defined; and circumstances can be imagined in which she might exercise a considerable influence upon her Prime Minister, if only by directing his attention not to her own views but to those of men of weight outside politics whom she might have consulted. She is, after all, necessarily a member of the Church of England, and a highly representative member, which neither the Prime Minister, nor the House of Commons to which he is responsible, need be.

Returning from this digression on the Church in the constitution, the new Bishops who appear on the Queen's engagement list come, as is commonly stated, to do homage. This is not quite accurate. Homage is an oath of unconditional submission: at the coronation a peer swears to become the Queen's man "of life and limb and of earthly worship"; and a bishop, once consecrated, cannot take it, because his first allegiance is to God. Instead, he swears "fealty", which is a medieval spelling of "fidelity", and in practice it is found that he is none the less a loyal subject for lack of the more drastically worded oath. Fealty is, of course, sworn only by bishops whose Sees are in

England, where the Church is established; but the Queen does not limit herself to receiving these, and nearly every prelate taking up his mission in some remote part of the Commonwealth may look forward to some conversation with his Sovereign before he embarks.

Other definite categories of important people who figure frequently in the engagement lists are new judges, who are invariably knighted and (unless knights already) would in any case have to come to receive the accolade; the higher officers of the Civil Service on taking over a new post; and most members of the Foreign Service who have reached the retiring age and attained a rank appropriate to their length of service.

With each and all of these various visitors, clerical and lay, military and civilian, her own subjects or from foreign lands, the Queen always passes quickly from the necessary formalities to direct discussion of the country or service with which the visitor is concerned. Nearly all of them go away surprised at the extent of knowledge of their special subjects that Her Majesty has revealed; and they generally conclude that she must have been reading it up before the interview. In fact the Queen does little or no "reading up" for these interviews; it is not to her taste, and anyhow she is much too busy to have time for it. (A royal tour oversea is another matter: for that she asks for a selection of books, and probably finds time to skim them on the voyage.) What is not appreciated by the occasional visitor is the way the Queen's interviews dovetail together and can be made to support one another.

The knowledge of Ruritania that surprises the new British Ambassador just leaving for that country does not come out of any book: it was picked up in conversation when the Ruritanian Ambassador in London came to present his credentials and stayed to luncheon, where the Duke of Edinburgh drew him out and the Queen listened. The missionary Bishop, bound for a half-savage African diocese, unexpectedly discovers that the Queen knows quite a lot about the menus served within recent memory at the cannibal feasts of his flock; he has failed to note that a distinguished cannibal chief's son, now transformed into a highly sophisticated Prime Minister, was in London for a Commonwealth conference last week, and was given every opportunity to entertain the Queen with memories of his childhood. The Queen, in short, has such a catholic acquaintance among *people* that her knowledge of *things*, which is probably greater than she herself realizes, comes to her unconsciously and is displayed without intention or effort.

To translate these general summaries into concrete form, it is perhaps now useful to examine the record of a short phase of the Queen's life, enumerating the highly miscellaneous functions that crop up from day to day. A varied sample may be obtained, for instance, from the months of June and July, 1954—months that need not be represented as particularly strenuous, since they include the Whitsun holiday and a selection of the functions both grave and gay that belong to the summer season.

In the middle of May the Queen and the Duke of Edinburgh had returned from their Commonwealth Tour round the world, of which more will need to be said presently. The first of June was a Tuesday, and on that day Vice-Admiral Powlett came to Buckingham Palace for the customary audience and informal conversation before taking up his appointment as Governor of Southern Rhodesia. The Lord Chamberlain attended to present the formal address of congratulation which by custom is presented to the Queen by the House of Lords after some memorable event like the Commonwealth Tour; a similar address from the House of Commons had been presented before the end of May. A delegation of members of the Parliament of France was in London to celebrate the fiftieth anniversary of the

Entente Cordiale; and the Queen entertained them to a cocktail party at Buckingham Palace, inviting a number of members of both Houses of the British Parliament, and other distinguished persons specially interested in Anglo-French relations to meet them. After they had gone she dined with the Duke of Edinburgh and spent the evening quietly at home. This is now their almost invariable habit whenever official engagements permit. They have learnt to set a high value on their limited opportunities for privacy, and reserve their visits to theatres and other entertainments, unless actually required of them for official reasons, for special occasions like family birthdays which seem to call for a party.

Wednesday, June 2, was Derby Day; and of course the great popular festival called for the presence of the Queen, for whom the great racing events in an exceptional degree combine duty with pleasure. (Critics who complain that she spends too much time at the races perhaps overlook that this is almost her only regular form of relaxation.) But before going to Epsom she had sat for a new series of studio photographs; and after returning she went to the Scala Theatre for a performance of the play *The Frog*, in which her sister and a number of other young amateurs were acting to raise funds for charity.

On Thursday Dr. Geyer, the outgoing High Commissioner for South Africa, came to the Palace to take leave. The Queen held a Privy Council for the ratification of some formal Government business; and in the afternoon the Prime Minister, Sir Winston Churchill, came to render one of his regular reports on affairs of state. Friday was in effect the beginning of the Whitsun holiday, and the Queen watched the Oaks before driving to Windsor to spend a few days off duty with her family and a few house guests.

Public business began again at the Palace on Whit Tuesday, June 8. The Queen gave her representative patronage to one of the secondary arts by attending the private view of the

Antique Dealers' Fair. The new Indonesian Ambassador was received with full diplomatic protocol. The Prime Minister was received in another brief audience. The new British Ambassador to La Paz came to be dubbed knight; and Sir Victor Mallet, lately Ambassador in Rome, took leave of the Queen on his retirement from the Foreign Service.

On June 9 the Queen was at Windsor again, where rehearsals for the annual ceremonies of the Order of the Garter were in progress; but she was in London again in the evening to take the salute at the Royal Tournament, in which picked teams from the three services annually display their prowess. Thursday, June 10, was her official birthday, when she presided over the traditional pageantry of Trooping the Colour on Horse Guards' Parade, and the Royal Air Force saluted her with a ceremonial fly-past as she stood on the balcony of Buckingham Palace to acknowledge their demonstration of efficiency and loyalty.

The engagements for June 11 include the separate reception of two senior diplomatists on their retirement from the Foreign Service, and the bestowal of the honour of knighthood on one of them. Later in the day the Queen with the sculptor and other experts inspected the model for the statue, afterwards erected overlooking the Mall, which forms the visible part of the national memorial to King George VI. Next day the hours to spare from the usual office work were divided between the reception of the High Commissioner for Pakistan and the Jubilee Review of the Royal Naval Volunteer Reserve, which had been founded by King Edward VII in 1904.

The following week was mostly spent at Windsor: it is one of the customary interludes in the royal year. On the Monday, June 14, the stately annual celebrations of the Most Noble Order of the Garter were held in the Castle. The Queen, as Sovereign of the Order, presided in the morning over the Chapter of the Order, in which new Knights are invested in their elaborate robes; entertained the Knights and their ladies to luncheon in St. George's Hall; and in the afternoon walked in procession to St. George's Chapel for the service of thanksgiving, in the course of which the new Knights are formally inducted into their stalls. On the Tuesday the Queen was entertained at a cocktail party by the officers of the Coldstream Guards, after investing the distinguished Windsor organist, Dr. William Harris, with the insignia of a Knight Commander of the Victorian Order; and the next two days were given up to Ascot Races, where the Queen annually takes her place as the leader simultaneously of sport and fashion, as she makes her daily entry driving in semi-state along the course. She paid a brief visit to Buckingham Palace on the Friday, in order to receive the Austrian Chancellor, who was on a visit to London, but was back at Windsor at the end of the week in honour of the fly-past of the Royal Air Force.

After this week of comparative relaxation—though it has to be remembered that the Queen had been "doing her boxes" even on Ascot days—that which followed was crowded with miscellaneous engagements. On June 22 the Queen started her list by presenting the Royal Victorian Medal to an old servant of the Household. Next came Sir Anthony Eden, the Foreign Secretary, to report to her on events in the diplomatic world. A deputation from the Loyal Regiment followed, with the gift of a brooch. Sir Oliver Harvey was then received on his retirement from the Paris Embassy and from the Foreign Service. The Prime Minister attended for his weekly audience and stayed to luncheon. In the afternoon, it being the eve of Alexandra Rose Day, a small group of ladies were admitted to the Palace to sell roses to the Household, and to the Queen, who spent a little time in conversation with them. And finally Sir Gladwyn Jebb, who was to succeed Sir Oliver Harvey in Paris, came to be invested with the Grand Cross of the Order of St. Michael and St. George.

The following day routine was varied by the arrival of a deputation from the Navy Club with a presentation for the Royal Yacht *Britannia*. The new Ambassador to Tokyo was received before leaving to take up his post, and then the Queen devoted what was left of the morning to a short sitting for her portrait in Mr. Simon Elwes's studio. On June 24 she received Mr. R. G. Casey, the Australian statesman, and the Lord Chamberlain came to transact some official Household business. A deputation from the Royal Numismatic Society was received on the occasion of their Jubilee. There followed a meeting of the Privy Council to enable the Queen to give her authority in the required legal form to certain acts of the Government; and the list of engagements ended with a presentation from the King's Royal Rifle Corps. On June 25 there was a change in the office of Comptroller of the Household, both the outgoing and the incoming dignitaries being received by the Queen; a deputation was received from the Royal Air Force Regiment; Sir Alfred Napier was received on his retirement from the position of Clerk of the Crown in Chancery and invested with the insignia of a Knight Commander of the Royal Victorian Order; and in the evening the Queen visited Australia House to see a newly completed film of the royal tour in the Commonwealth.

The closing days of the month were mainly occupied with the state visit of the King and Queen of Sweden, calling for elaborate exchanges of formal hospitality according to a traditional international pattern of which more will be said in another chapter. Besides these social events, the Queen gave an audience on June 30 to the Swedish Foreign Minister; and she found time, besides getting through her usual work at the desk, to give an audience to the Chancellor of the Exchequer and another sitting to Mr. Elwes, and to receive the Duke of Hamilton, who was to represent her as Lord High Commissioner at the annual General Assembly of the Church of Scotland—all these on June 29; and to say goodbye on June 30 to two diplomats on their retirement from the Foreign Service.

Leave-taking of the King and Queen of Sweden, the reception of a new Venezuelan Ambassador and an audience for the British Ambassador to St. Iago, the knighting of the new Governor of Cyprus and two more retirements from the Foreign Service filled in the interstices of routine at the end of that week and opened the month of July.

The first full week of that month brought Lord Ismay, Secretary-General of the North Atlantic Treaty Organization and Mrs. Pandit, High Commissioner for India, on successive days to the Palace, Lord Ismay staying to luncheon after his audience; it included an inspection of the Yeomen of the Guard, the Royal Show at Windsor and a tea party there for the tenants of Crown lands; the Lord Chamberlain came to discuss further Household business; the Queen gave a sitting to Mr. Elwes, received the representatives of the Southern Rhodesian Benevolent Fund, and took leave of another diplomatist retiring from the service; and the Canadian Ambassador to Greece came to see her on his way through London to take up his post.

The following week contained some considerable social functions: a garden party at Buckingham Palace, preceded by a presentation party for debutantes from oversea, and a dinner for the Queen as guest of honour of her Lord-Lieutenants of the counties of England and Wales. She held an investiture for some hundreds of men and women whose names had appeared in her Birthday Honours List; and the aged Mr. Somerset Maugham came separately to receive the insignia of a Companion of Honour. The Prime Minister came for one of his regular audiences, and the same day, Thursday July 15, the Queen held a Privy Council. Two newly appointed bishops did fealty, and Sir John Kennedy, retiring from the governorship of Southern Rhodesia, came to tell the Queen something about that country, which she had briefly visited as heiress presumptive seven years before. The

Master of the Queen's Musick was another caller. Industry was represented in the engagement list by a deputation of pottery manufacturers, and the Housing Exhibition just set up in Oxford Street by the Ministry of Housing was honoured with a visit from the Queen. The last recorded event of the week is the presentation of credentials by a new Ambassador from Bolivia.

Two of these events, the investiture and the garden party, were duplicated in the following week. There were sittings for two different artists. The Queen of the Netherlands and Prince Bernhard, who were on a private visit to England, came informally to luncheon. Once more there was an Ambassador to go through the ceremonies of inception—this time he was from Bulgaria. As head of the Army the Queen inspected the new uniforms designed for the Household troops, presented new colours to the Welch Fusiliers, appointed a new Aide-de-Camp General; and dined with her bodyguard of the Gentlemen at Arms—a body, four centuries old, of distinguished retired officers, nearly all generals, who escort her on great ceremonial occasions. The Foreign Secretary had an audience; and other visitors included the Commander of the British South African Police, and General Sir Gerald Templer who was laying down the office of High Commissioner in the Federation of Malaya and was shortly to take up that of Chief of the Imperial General Staff.

This was the end of the London season, and on July 24 the Queen left Buckingham Palace to spend a week as the guest of the Duke of Norfolk at Arundel Castle before going on with the Duke of Edinburgh for their summer holiday at Balmoral. But neither at Arundel nor at Balmoral was it ever possible for her entirely to shake off the burdens of her public position. Deputations came to Arundel on successive days to present loyal addresses on behalf of the two Houses of Parliament; and the closing business of the session required another Privy Council to be held at the castle, the Prime Minister being present and remaining to discuss affairs of state. Two Ministers came to surrender their seals on retirement from office—Sir Thomas Dugdale, Minister of Agriculture and Fisheries, and Mr. Oliver Lyttelton, Secretary of State for the Colonies, who on departure was to be raised to the peerage as Viscount Chandos. On the last day of July the Queen left Arundel and began her holiday journey north. But the red boxes, this year as always, would follow her all the way, and be with her until she returned to open Parliament in the autumn.

The Queen
in the United Kingdom

The Queen in the United Kingdom

A CCORDING to the theory of the English constitution since 1272, the Sovereign never dies: at the moment that a monarch draws his last breath the heir enters into the inheritance. On February 6, 1952, Queen Elizabeth II was instantaneously invested with the whole of the responsibilities of the representative kingship, as they had been borne by King George VI and as they have been outlined in the second chapter of this book. But she added to these a further responsibility, which has not hitherto been mentioned, because it was one from which her father by his sex was free. Taking over the many-sided task which was primarily designed for a man—and a hard-working man at that—she is not thereby relieved of the ordinary private duties of a woman.

England and the British Empire have thriven too mightily under the reigns of our great Queens to allow any doubt to remain of the desirability of the unusual social and political pattern that derives from the presence of a woman on the throne. But unusual it remains, and its exceptional character bears hardly upon the Queen herself. Burdens which centuries of experience have adjusted between the King and the Queen Consort have now to be redistributed unevenly. The Duke of Edinburgh has proved a tower of strength to his wife in many informal ways, giving on her behalf the support of his energetic and informed intelligence to everything that is most practical, forward-looking and masculine in the national life. But in the main work of the monarchy—not because of anything in the law but because of the nature of the people's feeling—he can do little or nothing. Not even in so masculine a sphere as the symbolic headship of the armed services would anyone but the Queen herself be acceptable. It goes without saying that in the strictly formal department of politics it would be quite unconstitutional for him to enter into any relationship with the business of government, except on the rare occasions when the Queen was absent from the realm, or ill, and had delegated her functions to him and other members of the Royal Family as Councillors of State.

In short, the presence of a devoted husband at her side, though it gives invaluable moral support, does not relieve the Queen of any substantial part of the labours that would be required of a King; while the distinctively feminine side of life, which her father and grandfather before her could leave unquestioningly to their Consorts, she must retain in her own hands. While playing a man's part in great affairs, she remains, as fully as any woman among her subjects, the wife, the mother, the hostess and the mistress of the house.

She is indeed the mistress of many houses. It is occasionally suggested that there are too many; but that question may be left for discussion in a later chapter devoted to the finance of the monarchy. For the present purpose it will suffice to mention what these various royal palaces are. Some of them belong to the Queen only in her symbolic capacity as representative of the nation; others provide her with homes in various parts of the kingdom.

In the first class the oldest and most important is the Palace of Westminster, where St. Edward the Confessor spent his last years in order to be near the Abbey that he had founded and in whose church he desired to be buried. It has been burnt down more than once, and the present building is wholly given over to the two Houses of Parliament. But it is still in theory the Queen's principal residence, to which from time to time she invites the notable men and women of her realm to "parley" with her. Her Throne stands there always (other thrones, in the Abbey or in Buckingham Palace, are only representations of this); she sits there as hostess to receive her guests at the state opening; and in token that this is indeed her house the supreme control of the establishment has been vested since 1133 in the hereditary Lord Great Chamberlain, that is, the head servant of her private apartments.

The Tower of London, almost as old as Westminster as a royal palace and older in respect of the buildings now standing on the site, has long since been handed over as a military head-quarters. But the Queen places her Crown jewels there for safe-keeping by her soldiers; and her personal relationship is affirmed every night in the ancient ceremony of saluting "Queen Elizabeth's Keys" as the chief warder goes his rounds at lock-up.

The third of the historic royal residences in London is now the theoretical headquarters, if not the home, of the Queen. Foreign Ambassadors are accredited "to the Court of St. James's". Certain dignified ceremonies, such as the presentation of loyal addresses by privileged bodies on such occasions as coronations or royal marriages, are transacted there. When levées were held for the presentation of male subjects to the King, this was their setting, and presumably will be again if the practice, interrupted since the beginning of the Second World War, is ever resumed—as is improbable. But in any case levées, when a Queen is on the Throne, are conducted by her Consort or by the Prince of Wales. St. James's is the meeting place of the Accession Council, which declares the name of the new Sovereign on a demise of the Crown, and his or her title is then proclaimed by the officers of arms from the balcony of the palace. But as a residence it has passed out of the Queen's personal occupation.

Certain large houses which are within its precinct but are not strictly part of it are assigned to important members of the royal family or to official uses—Clarence House to Queen Elizabeth the Queen Mother, York House to the Duke of

F

81

Gloucester, Lancaster House at present to Government hospitality. The Princess Royal has a suite of rooms in Friary Court. Much of the rest of the Palace is divided up into small "grace and favour" residences for private secretaries and other confidential servants of the Queen who work at Buckingham Palace; and the Lord Chamberlain, who is responsible for the ceremonial side of the work of the Royal Household (as distinct from state ceremonial, which is the responsibility first and foremost of the Earl Marshal) has there his office as well as his home. The Throne Room, Queen Anne's Drawing Room, and other state apartments, which are of great beauty and dignity, are occasionally used for banquets or exhibitions of royal association, and are sometimes lent by the Sovereign for the benefit of charitable causes. They were occupied, for example, throughout the Second World War by the departments of the Red Cross working on behalf of prisoners of war.

Two other houses are also split up mainly into "grace and favour" residences: Kensington Palace, the home of Queen Anne and of Queen Victoria when a child, chiefly for the use of the junior branches of the Royal Family, and Hampton Court, associated especially with Henry VIII, for aged servants of the Crown, principally distinguished officers in the armed services, or their widows, whose worldly wealth falls short of the measure of their deserts. All these residences, for which no rent is charged to the tenants, are in the personal gift of the Queen; but the administration of them is shared between the Office of Works and the Keeper of the Privy Purse and does not impose any further burden upon her.

She has also her palace of Holyroodhouse at Edinburgh, where her ancestors the Kings and Queens of Scots from the time of James IV kept their state; but this place of tragic memories is no longer in any but a formal sense a royal residence. It is indeed to Scotland very much what St. James's is to England. It is occupied during the annual meeting of the General Assembly of the Presbyterian Church of Scotland by the Queen's Lord High Commissioner, a political nominee who holds his court with considerable ceremony on her behalf; and occasionally the Queen herself may come and give a large garden party for the benefit of her Scottish subjects. But the Palace is now managed for her by public officials, and does not require her personal oversight.

It is quite otherwise with the four houses among which, when she is in the United Kingdom, her working hours, her home life and her holidays are divided. Historically, by far the most important of these is Windsor Castle, which was acquired by William the Conqueror from the Abbot of Westminster and has been the principal residence of the Sovereigns of England ever since. According to legend the Round Tower of the castle marks the spot where King Arthur and his knights set up their Round Table, in memory of which King Edward III instituted the Order of the Garter with Windsor as its home, so fusing the ideas of the Sovereign of the Order and the Sovereign of the Realm that the brotherhood of the Garter is in a sense interlocked with the very constitution itself. Consequently Windsor Castle is the scene of one of the two greatest ceremonies (the other is the state opening of Parliament) of the royal year—the procession of the Queen and her Red Cross Knights to their annual service of commemoration in St. George's Chapel, which will be more fully described in a later chapter. Windsor is the repository of the royal archives and library, and of the finest of the great royal collection of pictures—which are open to public view on most days of the year. Being within an hour's drive of London, it is constantly in use whenever the Queen has a day or two, generally at week-ends, to spend in the country. It is the natural place for her to entertain "house parties"; and she can often receive her official visitors there, politicians and others, with less distraction than in London. But except in June, when the Garter celebrations and Ascot races follow close upon one another, the Castle is seldom occupied for as much as a week at a time.

Buckingham House, the mansion of the Sheffield Dukes of Buckingham, was bought from them by George III and rebuilt so as to become, as Buckingham Palace, the main residential workshop of the monarchy. So it remains, having a population of officials and clerks suggestive of a small government department, but retaining throughout the character of a home, and one with a great tradition of hospitality to maintain. Secretaries, comptrollers, equerries, ladies in waiting, are all required from time to time to accompany their mistress wherever she may be, and they have their offices, as she has hers, in each of her houses; but this is their permanent headquarters, where those not in immediate attendance are to be found at work all the year round.

The other two houses are essentially holiday resorts, to be occupied when public business in London is in suspense, though there is no season of the year when the Queen's work can be wholly put aside. Balmoral Castle, in the county of Aberdeen, was bought by Queen Victoria and Prince Albert early in her reign and rebuilt in the ponderous "Scottish-baronial" style, which appeals little to twentieth-century taste. It provides however a much-loved centre for a summer holiday on the hills and moors of rural Scotland, and is of high value for the public significance of the monarchy in that it brings the Queen regularly to reside, with the minimum of formality, among her Scottish subjects. Sandringham House in Norfolk, a smaller and cosier establishment, was bought by Edward VII for Queen Alexandra, taking the place of Osborne House, the home of his mother's old age, which he presented to the nation. It is the most intimate of the royal homes, where the whole royal family generally assembles at Christmas, and from which the Queen, when in England, broadcasts her annual greetings to her peoples throughout her Commonwealth.

All these four houses are in their different measure back-grounds for the Queen's work, varying from the packed hour-to-hour calendar of Buckingham Palace to the skimming of off-season papers at Sandringham. But in all of them the Queen, before she turns to her public duties, has a private responsibility that a male Sovereign would escape: she has to "run the house". In each, of course, there is a considerable staff of servants, ranging from the Lord Steward to the pages and the kitchen-maids. But servants need to be supervised by the mistress of the house. She has to arrange her immense programme of enter-taining, and take the personal thought that only the hostess herself can give for the comfort and contentment of her guests. She is also a mother, anxious to give to her children every mo-ment that can be spared from her work, and no doubt worrying like other mothers over whether her daughter is sitting up too late with the television or her son is wearing his warm under-clothes at school. Such preoccupations as these make it more difficult for a woman than for a man to sustain the part of a public institution.

Against this background of domestic responsibility, then, the Queen has to organize her work of representing her peoples. Her first business, it cannot be too often repeated, is not to govern them. They govern themselves, according to a delicately balanced system in which she plays an indispensable but not a dominant part. Her first business is to know her people, to be known by them, and thereby to help them to know themselves. She has to associate herself with every worthy aspect of their activity, in order that by her participation all activities may be organically interlocked.

On the connecting door between the rooms of two of the Queen's private secretaries in the north wing of Buckingham Palace, so placed that it can be easily studied by either of them, hangs a map of Great Britain about a yard wide and a yard and a half high. This map is speckled with hundreds of coloured pins, like those used by strategists to mark the positions of friendly or hostile forces converging to battle: only these pins, once placed, are not moved again. Each pin indicates a visit paid by the Queen since her accession in 1952; the different colours distinguish the character of the visit, whether for a state function, an informal tour of factories, hospitals or schools, a sporting event, a holiday trip, or any other sort of journey. Naturally, the pins tend to "clot".

There is a thick cluster round London and Windsor, others near the great cities of the North; there are on the other hand some considerable spaces on the map that are still almost blank. But these bare patches are growing steadily fewer: it is the Queen's standing order to her Household staff that they are to be filled up as soon as possible. There will not, of course, ever be a time when the pins will be spread evenly over the map, if only for the obvious reason that the people are not spread evenly over the country: the more thickly an area is populated, or the more frequently events of national importance take place there, the more numerous the royal visits are likely to be. But the Queen is very insistent that it shall never appear that she is interested only in large conglomerations of people or in happenings on the national scale.

Country dwellers and local affairs "which have no meaning half a league away" are important in the Queen's eyes: she gives to the parish war memorial the meaning it bears for the parishioners. It is a fashionable criticism of the monarchy in the more self-consciously intellectual circles that far too much time is given to "laying foundation stones and things", functions which, it is argued, could be just as well performed by local dignitaries like lords lieutenant. That is emphatically not the Queen's view, because it is not the prevailing view of her subjects.

She is well aware, as she goes through a long series of local ceremonies, which seem infinitely monotonous to her entourage and to readers who follow her progress in the national newspapers, that for each separate community she visits there is the very reverse of monotony: her coming marks a red-letter day of intense excitement, long prepared for and lovingly remembered and discussed for long afterwards. If the lord lieutenant presides over the local celebration, it is an indication that it matters at most to the county; if the Queen herself takes the trouble to come, she is declaring that it matters to everyone. It is by such means that local patriotism is welded into the larger patriotism that supports a great nation; and it is for such reason that the Queen requires her staff so to manipulate the pins on their great map as to ensure that even the most stay-at-home of her subjects have a chance of seeing her in the flesh at reasonable intervals of time.

It is by no means easy to realize this ideal, for the local communities themselves would generally prefer that a royal visit should not come "out of the blue", but should be so timed as to fall upon a day important to themselves, when they have some event to commemorate, some enterprise to embark upon, or some achievement to set before the Queen and through her before the world. The organization of the Queen's movements about the kingdom must fit into the somewhat rigid framework set up by her calendar of necessary public functions in the capital; she will wish not only to visit every region with reasonable frequency but to appear there at the appropriate time. This is only to be achieved through the most elaborate staff-work by the small body of her personal servants, and incidentally by subtle diplomacy in trying to reconcile a multitude of conflicting claims.

Seen from the national point of view, which is also the Queen's own, all these visits are very much alike; from the local point of view only one matters, and that is unique. The editor of the local newspaper knows that he cannot possibly give his readers

too much about the events of the day. He turns on his whole
reporting staff and prints column after column of minute detail,
knowing that all will be avidly read by people eagerly searching
for mention, if not of themselves, then of people they know, in
immediate contact with the Queen. Her movements next day,
when she has gone to keep a very similar engagement in the next
county, interest him not at all. The national newspapers, on
the other hand, will give a short paragraph to each day's happenings; but since, in the absence of local contacts, one day is very
much like another, the whole series will be treated as a matter
of routine. Readers of neither class of newspaper have the
opportunity of seeing the programme as a whole in the detail
that will make clear the demands that it makes, over a period
of time, upon the principal actress.

Nor can the omission be corrected here. The local newspaper's reports of one day's royal visit to a moderate-sized town
would fill most of this book. Instead, it will be convenient to
look from the point of view of the Queen at the hour-to-hour
events of one or two of these visits; and then to survey the
Queen's annual calendar and see how much of it is filled with the
performance of similar duties. The first example, that of a
single-day visit to Winchester, is chosen because this ancient
city, the capital of England down to the Norman Conquest, is
to-day not only a county town with its apparatus of municipal
government, but also the see of one of the principal bishoprics
of the Church of England, the site of the oldest public school,
and the headquarters of two famous and closely connected
regiments, the King's Royal Rifle Corps, better known even
now by its old name of the 60th Rifles, and the Rifle Brigade.
When the Queen goes to Winchester she must take notice of all
these aspects of its life, and show appreciation of the compliments that the representatives of them all will wish to pay her.
The visit now to be considered was paid on July 25, 1955, when
the Sixtieth were celebrating the 200th anniversary of the

raising of the regiment in the New England Colonies, under the name of the Royal Americans, for service in the Seven Years War.

The day was a Monday, and the Queen and the Duke of Edinburgh had been spending the week-end at Broadlands, Lord Mountbatten's house in the New Forest, which seven years before had been lent to them for their honeymoon. They were therefore already within the county to be visited, and there was no occasion for the ancient courtesy whereby the Lord Lieutenant meets his Sovereign at the boundary when she enters his shire. This pleasant custom is of a piece with that whereby the Lord Mayor of London meets the Queen at Temple Bar whenever she comes to the City and surrenders the Sword (which is the sword of the Queen's Justice in the City, borne by him as her representative); and the Queen herself observes it when she goes in person to greet a visiting Sovereign at the terminus and drive with him to Buckingham Palace. But in a county context it does not easily fit the railway age, and from the time of George V has been generally dispensed with whenever it might cause even slight inconvenience. On the present occasion, as had been said, the question did not arise: the Lord Lieutenant of Hampshire, who was (and is) the Duke of Wellington, would await the Queen at her destination.

The Queen and the Duke of Edinburgh left Broadlands by motor car at half-past ten in the morning, accompanied by a lady in waiting, a private secretary, and an equerry. This is the usual strength of "attendance" prescribed by custom for ordinary visits; on occasions of state a considerably larger staff would be present, but for ornamental rather than practical purposes. For visits such as that to Winchester the little team of three would have plenty of practical work to do. Between them they may have spent weeks in planning the details of the day, including a time-table worked out precisely to the minute, and have been involved in much correspondence with the people and institutions to be visited, solving delicate questions about presentations and precedence, and allaying the anxieties and doubts of nervous local dignitaries desperately afraid of being tripped up by the imagined complications of royal etiquette.

One of the tests of an efficient Household officer is his ability to dispose of such preliminary perplexities—and he probably has plans for a whole season's functions in various stages of maturity at the same time—without troubling the Queen; but from time to time some question has to be referred for her personal decision. On the day, the three in attendance do not attempt, as they would on ceremonial occasions, to create an ornamental frame for the Queen, but hover discreetly in the background, looking for opportunities to help.

They are unobtrusively dressed, though if one of the fighting services is concerned in the programme the equerry on duty will usually be an officer in that service, and will appear in its uniform, as of course will the Duke of Edinburgh, who holds the highest rank in all three. Lord Plunket, who was the equerry in attendance at Winchester, was a captain in the Irish Guards. However, since this was a mixed military and civilian occasion, both the Duke and he started the day in plain clothes.

The journey by road from Broadlands took forty minutes, and at ten minutes past eleven the royal car arrived at Wolvesey Palace, the ancient residence of the bishops of Winchester adjoining the southern wall of the Cathedral Close. Here children from many local schools were drawn up in the grounds, and the Lord Lieutenant received the Queen and immediately presented the Mayor—who at this time was a lady, Mrs. Thackeray. The Lord Lieutenant and the Mayor in turn presented several leading personalities of the county and the city respectively, to each of whom the Queen said a few polite words —but very briefly, because only eight minutes could be allowed for the whole of the proceedings at Wolvesey, and, after the schoolchildren had sung the National Anthem, she wished to walk right down their long ranks, showing herself at close quarters to all, and stopping here and there to exchange a word with as many of them as time would allow. Punctually at eighteen minutes past eleven the Queen and the Duke were back in their car to go on to the next engagement.

This journey, made at a walking pace through the cheering crowds of children, was only the length of the Palace drive, for the gate of Wolvesey is almost opposite Outer Gate of Winchester College, where Sir George Gater, the Warden, was waiting to play host for the next stage of the day's proceedings. This famous school has been governed since 1387 by a body of ten fellows under a Warden—representing the eleven apostles without Judas Iscariot; and although none of these live in Winchester all but one had assembled to do honour to the Queen.

The Warden presented his nine colleagues together with his own wife and four of theirs, followed by the Headmaster, the Second Master, the Bursar and their ladies, all of whom followed in the wake of the Queen and the Duke as they crossed Outer Court to Middle Gate, which opens into Chamber Court, considered by all Wykehamists and many less biased judges the most beautiful medieval quadrangle in England. Here the whole school were drawn up in a hollow square within which Praefect of Hall, facing the Queen as she stood with the Warden and Headmaster in the archway of Middle Gate, addressed her in a Latin speech, according to the custom of welcoming distinguished visitors "Ad Portas" which can be traced back at least to the reign of Elizabeth I.

The Queen read a reply in English, in the course of which she asked the Warden and Fellows to add a few days to the summer holidays. This also is traditional for royal visitors, and always enhances the warmth of the three cheers that follow. Afterwards the Queen handed a Latin version of her speech to Praefect of Hall. It was an admirable piece of Ciceronian prose, but Her Majesty would scarcely require it to be represented as the product of her own classical scholarship. Though in quite recent times there has certainly been the ability close to the Sovereign to produce its like, the present writer dares to say, intending no offence to his friends in the Household, that this composition originated outside their ranks; it is even not improbable that it was constructed at Winchester itself.

This little ceremony was continued by the Queen's presentation to the winners of the gold medal for Latin prose and the silver medals for Latin and English speeches, which the Sovereigns of Great Britain from the time of George III have offered annually for competition at Winchester. This was a slight departure from tradition, for ordinarily the presentation is made by the Warden at "Medal Speaking" on the last day of the summer half. An example of one of the medals, dated rather a long time ago, lies before the author as he writes these words; and, remembering his own excitement at the age of seventeen merely because he was asked to send his medal back to Buckingham Palace to be inscribed with his name, he can imagine the thrill of these Wykehamists of another generation at receiving their awards from the hand of the royal donor herself.

It was now twenty minutes to twelve, and the next half-hour was spent in showing the Queen the chief beauties of the ancient college: Chapel, Cloisters and Fromond's Chantry, and Seventh Chamber, which of all the workrooms of College keeps most of its medieval aspect; and then the very lovely Memorial Cloister, built by Sir Herbert Baker to the honour of the hundreds of Wykehamists who were killed in the First World War. The last ten minutes were devoted to receiving the ten house-masters and their wives at the Headmaster's house, and at twenty minutes past twelve the royal car drove off. It was still only seventy minutes since the Queen had arrived at Winchester.

Now it was the turn of the civic authorities. At the Guildhall, in front of the statue of Winchester's greatest hero, King

Alfred the Great, erected to commemorate the thousandth anniversary of his death (unfortunately at a date since discovered to be two years out) a guard of honour was posted; and, after a royal salute, the Queen passed along the ranks with an occasional word for selected men. Then with the Duke she ascended the steps to meet the Mayor, who with formal words surrendered to her the symbol of civic authority, the municipal Mace. The Queen touched the Mace, in token that it existed for her service, and relinquished it as being well satisfied that it was in hands worthy of her trust.

The bewigged Recorder, who is the chief legal officer of the City and presides over its quarter sessions, read a loyal address, welcoming the Queen in brief and formal words to her faithful city, and the Queen with equal formality and even more briefly replied. The Mayor then presented her aldermen, councillors and others to the number of nineteen, and a little girl, with an elaborately rehearsed curtsey, placed a bouquet in the Queen's hands. (These flowers, which are apt to accumulate in embarrassing numbers on a long tour, are generally passed on to local hospitals after the Queen has carried them long enough to show her appreciation.)

The observances outside the Guildhall, including the inspection of the guard of honour, had been completed in ten minutes; and another quarter of an hour was now spent inside in showing the Queen and the Duke a collection of exhibits illustrating the sixty generations of Winchester's history, which had been brought together by the local antiquaries in honour of the occasion. At the end the mayor asked the Queen to accept an oak table as a present from the City to her two children, and a few more presentations of leading citizens filled up the five minutes remaining before sitting down to luncheon at one o'clock.

This, a comparatively informal meal without speeches, lasted an hour and a quarter, and then a short run of five minutes took the royal party from the civil to the military environment at the Green Jackets Depot, where the Queen was received by the two Colonels Commandant of the Sixtieth Rifles, General Sir Evelyn Barker and Lieutenant-General Sir Euan Miller. She spent twenty-five minutes with these two distinguished officers absorbing something of the history of the Sixtieth in the regimental museum, which gave time for the Duke of Edinburgh to change into Field Marshal's uniform in the Officers' Mess. A drive of about two miles along the Southampton Road to St. Cross brought them to the parade ground for the main business of the day.

A formal military review always proceeds on the same lines, though this was a very exceptional occasion, remarkable not only for the muster of the full active strength of the regiment, but for the presence among the spectators of a great number of its retired members, headed by the Prime Minister, Sir Anthony Eden, who had been a rifleman in the First World War and won the Military Cross while serving with the regiment in France. According to custom the Queen was received with a Royal Salute, and then inspected the entire parade: that is, she passed slowly along the stationary ranks of all units, attended by the Colonels Commandant and battalion commanders with drawn swords. Having completed the inspection she took her place at the saluting base, where General Barker delivered a speech of welcome, and the Queen addressed him and the regiment in reply. Both speeches naturally dwelt upon the great fighting traditions of the regiment in the service of the Queen's ancestors, and on the determination of the officers and men now serving to continue them worthily, the Queen especially complimenting all concerned on the fine bearing of the men she had just seen.

On occasions such as this nobody should, of course, imagine that the Queen speaks out of her personal knowledge: she is generally making her first direct acquaintance with the institution she honours, and she must rely for her facts upon the people who know them. Her speech is always a co-operative production. The authorities of the regiment—or the society, the hospital, the factory, the college—send the raw material well in advance to Buckingham Palace, giving the facts about the institution to be visited and drawing attention to such achievements, hopes, or difficulties as in their judgment it would be timely to emphasize. This material is then moulded into the form of a speech by one of the royal private secretaries. Sometimes more than one will take a hand; very occasionally, if there is any possibility that public policy may be involved, a Government Department may have to be consulted, for if anything the Queen says is challenged, no matter how informal the circumstances in which she speaks, her Ministers may be held responsible in Parliament. That is the British Constitution.

For example, if the commanding officer of a regiment about to be inspected expressed the hope that the Queen may make some allusion to the famous victory in 1758, when the regiment unsupported put the entire Laputan army to flight, the private secretary, who knows that the negotiations for a commercial treaty with Laputa are just reaching a delicate phase, may think it necessary to get a memorandum from the Foreign Office for the Queen, advising her on how much it would be prudent to say. For prudence is the indispensable quality of the Sovereign's public utterances. Unlike her Consort, who can legitimately allow himself far more latitude because he speaks for himself alone, she must never take the risk of making a mistake. To those of her critics who find her speeches over-conventional, the answer is that she has no choice but to play for safety. That also is the British Constitution.

The draft speech is eventually submitted to the Queen, who whether she accepts the text as it stands or wishes to make her own emendations in it, will probably wish to discuss it with her staff and will invariably spend some time studying it in order to prepare herself for reading it effectively in public. In this she gains a preliminary impression of the regiment or other institution she is going to visit, to be corrected and amplified by her personal contacts on the day. In a word, the composition of royal speeches probably contributes at least as much to the progressive education of the Queen herself as to the edification of her audience.

After the speeches the units on parade, to the music of the regimental band, marched past in column of companies in quick time—which for a rifle regiment is quicker by twenty paces to the minute than for ordinary infantry—and then again in close column in double time, each company giving the salute "eyes right" on passing the Queen and the officers saluting with their swords. Then the whole parade re-formed in line and advanced to give the final royal salute, ending with three cheers for the Queen before marching off.

The main body of troops having departed, the Prime Minister, the Chief of the Imperial General Staff, Sir John (now Lord) Harding, and the principal officers of the regiment remained for a few minutes' conversation with the Queen. They included the Colonel Commandant of the sister regiment, the Rifle Brigade; the oldest rifleman, Lord Penrhyn; a Boer War V.C., Major-General Price Davies; and the commanders of the regimental depot, the two regular battalions, and the associated territorial units. There were also present five American citizens who had crossed the Atlantic on purpose for the occasion. They were men who had joined the regiment at the beginning of the Second World War, and had served with it so long as their own country remained neutral. After the United States entered the war they were released to join the American forces. Many of the British officers, and two of the Americans, had brought their wives, who were included in the presentations.

The Old Comrades of the regiment, in civilian dress but wearing their medals, had remained on the parade ground, and the Queen now spent ten minutes inspecting their ranks and engaging a few veterans of three wars in conversation; and then over tea she received still more presentations of officers, non-commissioned officers and men, taking her place in the middle of a group of officers, warrant officers and N.C.O.s to be photographed before leaving St. Cross at a quarter to five. That is to say, including the visit to the depot, she had devoted two hours and twenty-five minutes to the military part of the day's cele-brations.

After the municipality, education, and the army, there was only half an hour left for the church. But during that time the Queen was able to meet the Bishop and the Dean at the great west door of the Cathedral, and to receive the presentation of the four canons, two of whom were suffragan bishops, and the wives of the Dean and the Bishop of Southampton, and to show herself to a gathering of workers associated with the Cathedral, fifteen of whom were also presented. After signing the visitors' book she and the Duke of Edinburgh left by the South Nave door through ranks of boys and girls from the private schools in and near Winchester. In her transit between the West and South doors she had been taken by the Dean on a necessarily hasty tour of one of the most magnificent churches in England, where lie the bones of an unknown number of her predecessors, collected anonymously into chests after being scattered by sacrilegious hands, and where an austere tomb in the middle of the nave, without ornament or inscription, is commonly believed to cover the remains of King William II, called Rufus. Here also Richard Coeur de Lion was crowned for a second time after his return from captivity in 1194, and Queen Mary Tudor was married in 1553. And here are monuments to many famous historical figures of contrasted greatness: Joan of Arc and Cardinal Beaufort who presided over her burning; William of Wykeham and Jane Austen.

It was now half-past five, and at the Deanery, which stands in the Cathedral Close, the Queen spent twenty-five minutes in conversation with Sir Anthony Eden, while the Duke of Edinburgh was getting back into civilian dress. The Prime Minister had requested an audience in order to lay business of state before his Sovereign; but such matters belong to another aspect of the Queen's function, which has no place in a chapter devoted to illustrating her position as the social head of her people. An hour's run from the Deanery brought the royal party to Goodwood House, where they were to dine and stay as the guests of the Duke and Duchess of Richmond.

The whole programme, from leaving Broadlands to the arrival at Goodwood, had taken about eight and a half hours: a full day's work, though not an excessively long one. In that space of time the Queen had listened to two speeches and made two herself; had given audience to her chief Minister; had made or renewed the acquaintance of well over a hundred of her subjects; had shown herself to many thousands more; had viewed three outstanding ancient buildings and two modern museums; and had played her part in the life of four great corporate institutions—a municipality, a public school, a regiment, and a cathedral chapter.

It was indeed a crowded programme, yet only one in a succession of such programmes by which the Queen extends her knowledge of the country over which she presides. It has been worth while examining it in considerable detail here if the result is to convey an idea of the ingenuity with which the Queen's time is disposed so as to extract the maximum of public utility from every fleeting minute. It is only by this extreme economy of time that the necessary duties are packed into the day, and into day after day, without risk of overtiring the principal character. It is above all things necessary that the Queen shall not be physically exhausted, not for her own sake (there is no doubt of her willingness to wear herself out in the public service if necessary) but for the sake of the function she has to discharge.

She needs to bring an air of freshness and vitality to the last as as well as the first of the changing audiences she will confront in the course of a long day; to betray a sense of strain would be as much an element of failure as it would be in an actress on the stage when strain is not in the part she has to play. The Queen in fact prides herself, and rightly, on her ability to go through all her duties without showing signs of fatigue; but even her splendid resilience might not be equal to the test without the constant diligence of her staff in sparing her any expenditure of effort that could possibly be wasteful.

Winchester, perhaps beyond any other city in the land, takes its character from ancient tradition. By way of contrast to the day spent there let us now look, a little less minutely, at a slightly longer royal visit to a busy centre of the most modern industry. The occasion is the tour of parts of Worcestershire, Herefordshire and the Forest of Dean on Tuesday and Wednesday, April 23 and 24, 1957.

This was one of the frequent journeys that are made in the royal train. That the Queen should possess such a train is eminently suitable, for the railways are her property. Indeed, in the Union of South Africa, where she also owns the railways, there is a personal saloon and sleeping car allotted to every Minister, which he has attached to any train he pleases when he wishes to travel. The Queen herself can and often does use ordinary trains when passing from one to another of the royal residences, particularly between Balmoral and Buckingham Palace or Windsor. The special usefulness of the royal train is for occasions when she has to spend one or more nights away from home; for then she can avoid imposing upon anybody's hospitality.

Far back in English history, in days when the whole government followed the King on his movements about the realm— and before anyone had thought of taxation as a means of financing the State—the whole court, administrators, judges, household officials, soldiers, and a horde of hangers-on used to descend on a locality like a swarm of locusts and eat up its resources until the imminence of local famine compelled it to move on. This was almost the only way that the King and his retinue could subsist; and the remains of the system, under the name of purveyance, were still a bone of contention between Charles I and his Parliaments. Even as late as the reign of Elizabeth I entertaining the Queen and her court, though in theory voluntary, was a moral duty for the higher nobility (hence the innumerable beds in which the Queen is said to have slept); and more than one great figure in his county ruined himself by his ostentatious expenditure on a single royal visit.

Though Sovereigns from Queen Victoria onwards have dispensed with the enormous retinues thought necessary to sustain the dignity of their predecessors, something of the tradition survived into very recent years. George VI, however, set his face against it, even before wartime rationing made its continuance impossible. He and his daughter after him ceased to stay in the houses of anyone but their personal friends; they would not demand of the Lord Lieutenant or anybody else to entertain them as a matter of official duty. However much they might express contentment with the simple style of living that both of them genuinely preferred, they knew very well that no public dignitary would feel happy in entertaining his Sovereign on less than a princely scale. Moreover, personal and county pride would become involved, and competition, wasteful and burdensome, would be inevitable.

The answer to the dilemma was the royal train. It is equipped with sleeping cabins and bathrooms, workrooms, kitchen and dining saloons for the royal family and such small staff as they are likely to take with them; and it can be connected by telephone with the local exchange at every halt. By its use the Queen can carry on her various functions almost as if she were at home—in fact she is at home—without being beholden to anyone. The only disadvantage is that four hundred years hence the house-proud people announcing "Elizabeth II slept here" will be either few or fraudulent.

For the functions now to be summarized the royal train picked up the Queen and the Duke of Edinburgh at Windsor station after dinner on Monday and, after a short night run of three hours, was halted in the small hours of the morning in a siding at Leigh Court, a few miles out of Worcester to the west. The usual staff, of lady in waiting, assistant private secretary and equerry, were in attendance.

The party breakfasted in the train, and while the Queen made her usual morning study of the newspapers and dealt with any matters of urgency that had been reported to her private secretary by telephone or post since leaving Windsor, another run of three quarters of an hour brought them to Hagley, which is rather nearer to Birmingham than to Worcester, but still in the county. Here Admiral Sir William Tennant, as Her Majesty's Lieutenant for Worcestershire, was waiting on the platform to receive her into the county, where, it has always to be remembered, he holds the same position as the Sovereign herself holds in the realm, as its social head but not its active ruler. He had with him a party of nine or ten people—the sheriff, the chief constable, the chairman of the rural district council and others—to present to the Queen before she left by car for the first industrial visit on the programme.

This was to the heavy engineering firm of Walter Somers Ltd. Once more there were presentations. The Lord Lieutenant presented the mayor and the mayor presented the mayoress, the town clerk and the councillors; he also presented Mr. Frank Somers, the head of the firm, who in turn presented his directors. It was quite a large party that then accompanied the Queen on her tour of the works, which lasted about an hour. It was followed by a half-hour's visit to the Council House at Oldbury, a town whose industrial interests are largely concerned with the rare metallic element called titanium.

There were of course the usual civic presentations. It is possible that the Queen had hitherto possessed a very hazy idea of what titanium was; but she was given an object lesson in its versatile uses when the mayor presented to her a rose bowl and to the Duke of Edinburgh a shooting stick, both made of the same recondite substance. After taking coffee with the mayor the party drove on to Rowley Regis, where (taking the presentations as read) the main purpose was to give a sight of the Queen to hosts of schoolchildren, assembled round a dais that had been built for her by the side of the road. Having signed the visitors' book, and carrying the bouquet presented by one of the children, she went on to Dudley, walked through a hundred yards of more schoolchildren, and received no fewer than eighty presentations on the Council House steps. It was now one o'clock, and the Queen and the Duke had fairly earned their luncheon, which they took as guests of the Council, and from which they brought away mementos of the town's leather industry, in the form of a handbag and photograph frames given them by the mayor.

The first part of the afternoon was given to the study of the glass industry, both in the Brierley Hill glassworks, where the intricate processes of cutting, engraving and polishing glass were explained to the Queen, and at the glass exhibition which had been organized in the Council House at Stourbridge. The long list of presentations included not only the "bigwigs", but a nonagenarian glass cutter, now retired, who had given 63 years service to Brierley Hill as well as 25 to the volunteer and reserve forces of his country, and a former director of 87, who was distinguished as a cameo artist and had served for 60 years. At the works the Queen was given a set of cut-glass vases, and at the exhibition engraved cocktail glasses and a mixer.

At Kidderminster there was time only to meet the mayor and

civic personalities over tea in the town hall; but the Queen accepted two of the famous carpets to remind her of the town's most important industry, and left behind, with her signature in the visitors' book, a number of signed photographs of herself. It was now half-past five. The royal train had been brought to Kidderminster to pick up the party, and they were allowed a breathing space of nearly two hours and a half, during which it was halted at Droitwich Spa and the Queen and the Duke had a quiet dinner by themselves.

But this was by no means the end of the day. After dinner the train steamed off again and arrived at a quarter to nine at Shrub Hill station in the city of Worcester. This time there was no ceremony at the station, where the railway officials did all that was necessary to receive the Queen and see her into her car to attend a full dress reception at the Guildhall. She was received there by the Secretary of State for Air, Mr. G. R. Ward, who was (and is) the Member of Parliament for Worcester, the Mayoress and the Chairman of the County Council. Half the guests were gathered in the hall and the other half in the assembly room on the floor above; and, after receiving twenty-three presentations representative of both the city and the county, the Queen devoted a strictly rationed half-hour to circulating in each of the two rooms for informal conversation with as many guests as could be crowded into so short a space.

At five minutes past ten she was able to sit down for a little while in the Mayor's Parlour, where a deputation of field officers from the Queen's Own Worcestershire Hussars brought her the regiment's gift of a brooch, and the Mayor gave her a pair of gloves, locally manufactured. Rejoining the royal train at twenty minutes to eleven, she was back at Leigh Court just before eleven o'clock, having been engaged in or travelling between public functions for close on fourteen hours of the day, apart from the two and a half hours spent at Droitwich Spa over dinner and dressing for the Guildhall reception.

The second day of the expedition began with a few further functions in Worcestershire: first a quick survey of the troops in garrison on the county cricket ground at Henwick, to which the royal train had been driven at ten o'clock. There was time only for a few presentations of senior officers, a royal salute and inspection of the guard of honour and the old comrades, and then a drive round the troops on parade in a Land-Rover. By five minutes to eleven the Queen was being received by the Minister of Supply at Malvern, where (after presentations) she made a cursory tour of the laboratory and engineering workshops of the College of Electronics. This was all over in twenty minutes, and, after a drive through the streets of Malvern, lined with great crowds to see the royal car go by, the party arrived at twenty minutes to twelve at the Government's Radar Research Establishment. Fifty minutes were spent here, first in listening to an explanation by the director of the complex and largely secret processes in which the establishment was engaged, and then in watching a demonstration of the equipment of guided weapons and further demonstrations of technical processes in the laboratories of the radar and physics department. At half-past twelve the royal car was on the road again, and the visit to Worcestershire was over.

The visit to Herefordshire was in the nature of an epilogue, having to be compressed into a long afternoon, and leaving the county with a strong claim to more leisurely royal attention at some future date. The Lord Lieutenant and his wife met the party immediately after crossing the border, accompanied them to Ledbury, where the first batch of presentations was made, and were invited to luncheon with the Queen and the Duke of Edinburgh in the royal train, while in transit from Ledbury to Leominster. Here there was a commemorative plaque to be unveiled at the municipal offices; and both the Queen and the Duke planted oak saplings on Dinmore Hill. At Hereford the children of the city had been assembled on the athletic ground to sing the National Anthem, and the Queen and the Duke drove round their ranks in a Land-Rover, accepting a bouquet—not the first of the afternoon—half way round the circle.

In this great farming county the characteristic episode of the day was the visit to the cattle market, where the Queen and the Duke were presented with cider mugs on behalf of the apple growers of Herefordshire and watched a parade of Hereford cattle and Ryelands sheep. The denizens of the neighbouring pig market are not so good at ceremonial manœuvre, but came in none the less for their share of royal attention.

Before tea in the Town Hall the Queen inspected a guard of honour, and met the Bishop, the Garrison Commander, the Mayor, the Recorder and other leading citizens of Hereford. (It goes without saying that presentations had been made at each previous halt along the way.) She unveiled another commemorative plaque and passed on to the Cathedral, the historic beauties and treasured possessions of which were displayed to her by the Dean, after he had presented the members of the Chapter and others of its fellowship, both clerical and lay. Though every English cathedral has its own strongly marked individuality, the programme for the Queen's visit was necessarily on much the same lines as it had been at Winchester; but this time she was present at an act of worship, the singing of the Easter carol; and after signing the visitors' book she was given a model of one of the cathedral's most famous relics, called "King Stephen's Chair". Leaving the cathedral at half-past five, the Queen and the Duke paused for three quarters of an hour at Ross-on-Wye to meet the members of the Urban District Council, and after a half-hour's drive to the Severn Estuary at Beachley, which they crossed by the ferry boat, arrived at a quarter past eight at Badminton, where they were to be the guests of the Duke of Beaufort and his Duchess, who is the Queen's cousin.

Looking back now over the episodes of these three entirely characteristic days, one or two features are noticeable. One is the very large number of presentations: if the Queen averages fewer than a hundred a day she is having an easy time. Moreover, the people presented have a considerable family likeness. Mayors and councillors, deans and canons, colonels and field officers, chairmen and directors: from the Queen's point of view they are all very much alike, respectable public figures in a small way. From the local point of view, however, they bulk a great deal larger: they are the heads of the community, its natural representatives to the Queen, who is herself the representative of the larger, national, community of which theirs is a part. They are the people who have "made good" in the county or the city; and if the list of them is to be cut down in order to allow a larger selection of more ordinary people to meet the Queen, there will be bitter complaints that success in life, and good service to the Commonwealth, is denied its legitimate recognition.

Since there are only twenty-four hours in a royal day, there is really no way of getting round this dilemma. But it means, among other things, that since the persons chosen to be presented to the Queen are, in the overwhelming majority, the men and women who have "arrived", it is almost impossible on these occasions for a young Sovereign to make real contact with local people of her own age.

She does her best, by singling out the recruit on parade or the apprentice at the work bench for the exchange of a dozen words or so; but inevitably she must hasten on to keep to the time-table. Day after day she finds herself sitting at the luncheon or dinner table between a white-haired mayor and a septua-genarian bishop or admiral. They are always altogether admirable people, on their best behaviour; and the Queen, who for her years is already an old hand at this sort of thing, draws them out to enlighten her on every subject within their special knowledge, for the ultimate enrichment of her receptive and tidy memory. But she must sometimes sigh for the opportunity, on these semi-official tours, to look a little deeper into the thoughts of some of her own contemporaries.

Another feature of these tours is the accumulation of gifts that loyalty insists upon offering to the Queen. She has never, perhaps, even on her wedding day, surpassed the three tons of presents that the Duke and Duchess of York brought back to their daughter's nursery from their tour of Australia and New Zealand in 1927; but even on those two days in Worcestershire and Herefordshire she and the Duke, as has been seen, collected (besides a number of bouquets), a rose bowl, a shooting stick, a handbag, two photograph frames, some cut glass vases, a set of cocktail glasses and mixer, two carpets, a pair of cider mugs, and a model of King Stephen's Chair.

In the course of a year's travels these acquisitions mount up to a very substantial total. Their value is chiefly sentimental —on the side of both givers and receiver. We have travelled a long way from the court of Queen Elizabeth I, where everybody, from Lord Burghley and Lord Leicester down to the pages, was expected to make the Queen a New Year present of a scheduled value, on a sliding scale according to his rank, and received in return a piece of the royal plate, worth considerably less. (Thus was brought together the vast accumulation of silver which was ultimately melted down into coin to pay the troops of King Charles I in the Civil War.) The modern custom is maintained mainly by corporate bodies, for the Queen does not accept presents from individuals who are not her personal friends. But since the offerings are nearly all the products of local industry, their presentation nourishes the pride of the community in its labour and skill, and causes a high compliment to be paid to the particular craftsman whose work is singled out as worthy of the Queen's acceptance.

On her side, it may well seem *a priori* that she must be storing up a large herd of "white elephants". She does not, however, so regard them. They have all been laid before her as tokens of the affection in which she is held by her subjects; and their gradual amassing over the years endows her with a uniquely representative collection of all the best that her people can achieve, capable of summoning up reminders of innumerable pleasant occasions. Her home, in the result, comes to contain a sort of informal museum of British industry; and one is tempted to wonder whether an occasional exhibition of the gifts presented during the year, or during the whole reign up to date, might not have the same sort of popular appeal as the show of her wedding presents at St. James's Palace ten years ago.

There are, of course, many types of institution or activity which do not happen to have a place in the programme of these three days. In the first five years of her reign, for example, the Queen made prolonged tours of fifteen hospitals, distributed from Norwich to Chester and from Midhurst to South Uist. Three of these were children's hospitals, one of them, at Banstead in Surrey, dedicated in her name. Visiting the sick is, of course, a traditional royal occupation, and many hospitals have members of the royal family as their presidents or patrons, who take a constant interest in their affairs, as Princess Elizabeth, before her accession, did in the affairs of those with which she was associated. Similarly, the Queen has lately begun a study of the state school system, following a programme that will enable her, in the course of the next two years, to acquaint herself with every type of maintained school.

These visits are very thorough inspections. On one of the first of them, for example, to Queen Elizabeth's Girls' Grammar School at Barnet, the Queen saw every class at work, and incidentally made her first short speech without notes—chiefly memorable to its hearers because she asked for two days' holiday. This was a characteristic occasion, in that the only mention in the press was the report that the head girl had presented the Queen with a doll for Princess Anne. Nor indeed is there any reason why the national newspapers should take any interest in such monotonously repeated events. Their local importance, however, in the lives of small communities whose self-esteem is suddenly, enormously, and healthily inflated by the presence of the Sovereign, can hardly be over-estimated.

Nothing in the annual round of royal duties is considered more important than this business of making contact with the people in their home towns and at their work. The Queen resolutely refuses to have it reduced to mechanical routine; if in any way possible she prepares carefully in advance for every visit, reading up the history of the place to which she is going or the regiment she is to inspect, and seeking opportunities of conversation with anybody available in London or at Windsor who knows the region and can give her hints. She demands to see the time-table beforehand, and goes carefully through it line by line, rather priding herself on her ability to detect impossibilities that have escaped subordinate eyes. There is a long-standing family competition between the Queen Mother and her daughter to see which can get through the longest programme of public appearances. But in fact the scales are heavily loaded against the Queen by the multitude of inescapable daily duties that she must perform behind the scenes. It is indeed excessively difficult to find any free days on which the Queen can show herself to people who do not live near any of her homes.

Part of the difficulty lies in the fact that not all of the year is or could be made available for this purpose. The public work of the Queen is concentrated, so to speak, into two terms. The summer term runs from the beginning of February to the end of July or the first days of August; the winter term occupies the three months from October to Christmas. The summer term includes an interval of about six weeks, covering Easter, during which the Queen is at Windsor, but in close touch with Buckingham Palace and able to attend to any business requiring her presence there. It is therefore perfectly true that she takes longer holidays than the general run of her subjects, if a holiday is taken to mean any period spent away from one's usual place of work. It will appear in a later chapter that the Queen's apparently long holidays do not give her at any time that complete suspension of ordinary cares which most of us take for granted. But if their mere calendar length is to be the occasion of criticism, two considerations have to be taken into account.

First, it is not the purpose or justification of the monarchy that the Sovereign shall be ceaselessly active. Her significance as the universal representative, the focus of unity for kingdom and Commonwealth, resides in what she is and not in what she does; though of course what she is involves her in the doing of a very great number and diversity of things. In tranquillity as well as in visible action she is still the Queen.

The second consideration, directly relevant to the theme of this chapter, is that the sacrifice of her holidays would not enlarge her opportunities of attendance at public functions. Nearly all such functions are necessarily arranged during the busy times of the year, and could not be otherwise organized. It is not practicable to make a royal visit to a school during the summer holidays, to the Chelsea Flower Show in mid-winter, or to a regiment in the camping season. If the Queen spent Christmas in London she would find it deserted of most of the people she needed to see; and if she went on progress through an industrial area in August, she would dislocate the holidays of innumerable functionaries who would feel bound to give up their own vacation in order to attend upon her.

Thus the three months spent at Sandringham and Windsor would in any case be impossible for the undertaking of any substantial programme in Great Britain (it will presently be seen that they have sometimes been turned to account in the service of the Commonwealth); the six weeks at Windsor are thickly studded with engagements. In addition, it is regarded as essential that the Queen shall be within easy reach of London as long as Parliament is sitting.

In the light of these observations we may now survey the list of royal engagements for the most recent complete year—1957. It will not be found to conform entirely to the normal pattern; but no year ever does. There is always something to cause divergence. In this case irregularities began right at the beginning, with the arrival of Sir Anthony and Lady Eden at Sandringham on the afternoon of January 8. This was the first publicly notified episode in the train of events that brought about Sir Anthony's resignation of the office of Prime Minister, and the installation of a new Government under Mr. Harold Macmillan. Actually, Sir Anthony left Sandringham in the morning of January 9, and the Queen followed him to London in the afternoon, in order to receive the formal surrender of his charge at Buckingham Palace. The consultations, councils, leave-takings, and admissions of new Ministers to office caused the Queen to make several more journeys to London during the month; and in addition the death of her great-uncle, Lord Athlone, was followed by a state funeral at Windsor, and sent the court into mourning. Even so, this holiday month—as it should have been—included one or two small functions in the neighbourhood of Sandringham, where King George V took very seriously his position as the local squire, and his son and grand-daughter have been careful to preserve the tradition. For example, in between two interviews with her new Prime Minister on Thursday the tenth and Sunday the thirteenth, the Queen presented Sunday School prizes at West Newton on the Saturday and received the prize pupil from Dersingham School, to whom she gave a Bible, before catching the afternoon train to London on the Sunday.

The first half of February saw the Queen closely tied to London by a long series of engagements of a kind that have been discussed in an earlier chapter; and on the sixteenth she left England by air for the state visit to Portugal, and incidentally for her own reunion with the Duke of Edinburgh, who was on his way home from Australia and was to meet her on Portuguese soil. By the time they landed again at London Airport there was less than a week of February left, and that was very full of routine duties. But the engagement book does include one entry that deserves a passing mention, since it falls within the subject-matter of "getting to know the people", which is the theme of the present chapter. On Wednesday, February 27 the Queen and the Duke of Edinburgh gave a private luncheon party at Buckingham Palace.

These parties, which are an innovation of the present reign, have come to take an important place in the pattern of royal life. Their purpose is to bring into the Queen's presence, on easy and informal terms, notable men and women whose particular distinction does not qualify them to be received in any official capacity. There are generally about a dozen guests; and in order that as many interesting people as possible may be brought into personal contact with the Queen, the social convention that husbands and wives are always invited together is suspended. If both husband and wife have separate distinction of the kind that would qualify them for an invitation, the couple may be asked to a royal dinner party; but these are less frequent and rather more formal functions.

To the luncheons come men and women from every walk of life, not necessarily of great eminence, but all people who have made sufficient mark to distinguish them as individuals, and who are able to open a window for the Queen on some corner of the infinitely various life of the nation over which she presides. Artists, scholars, writers, and musicians, leaders of industry and trade-union officials, scientists and explorers, lawyers, magistrates, social workers, clergymen of any denomination, actors, athletes, sportsmen—in fact, representatives of every calling—mingle almost haphazard at the Queen's table, and are encouraged to talk freely with one another and with her, contributing thereby to her deeper understanding of her people, and receiving assurance that the activities for which they stand are no less important in her eyes, and therefore in the eyes of the country, than those of the official or political world. Not that politicians and officials are excluded from the parties; but they are there in their personal capacity, to round off and complete the representation of all sorts and conditions of the Queen's subjects, and not as cogs in the machinery of the State.

It goes without saying that those who are invited are chosen without regard to party allegiance; for though the Queen may take advice only from that party which has for the time being the confidence of the House of Commons, in private life members of all parties are equally her friends, and these luncheons are private and social occasions. Conservatives, Labour men and Liberals meet at their royal hostess's board as friends of hers and therefore of one another's. For this reason the existence of the monarchy helps to preserve the tolerant and courteous tone of human intercourse between political opponents which has for centuries been characteristic of British public life, and especially of the life of Parliament—which meets, it is to be remembered, at the Queen's summons and in a royal palace.

Returning from this digression to the main line of the Queen's public engagements, we have now reached the month of March. It began that year on a Friday, and the Queen and the Duke of Edinburgh spent that day in viewing the complex and largely secret work in atomic research in progress at Harwell. The following Monday they were shown round the *Daily Mail* "Ideal Home" exhibition at Olympia, in West London; and on the Tuesday, after an Investiture in the morning, they paid a visit to Harrow School. This was widely interpreted as a pointer to their thoughts in the matter of the Duke of Cornwall's [1] education, and no doubt, like any other parents, they had the

[1] Now the Prince of Wales.

future of their own son in their minds as they were shown the routine of the place and talked to the Headmaster and others about their work. But the Duke of Cornwall was at the time still at his "pre-preparatory" school, and there is no special reason to suppose that Harrow, which, as has already been shown in this chapter, was not the first great public school they had visited and will certainly not be the last, should be regarded as anything but one of several possibilities.

The rest of that week was full of official engagements, and so was the whole of the next; so that, except for another Buckingham Palace luncheon and a dinner party, there was no other event falling within the scope of this chapter until Saturday, March 16, when the Queen and the Duke of Edinburgh went to Twickenham to see the match for the Calcutta Cup between England and Scotland, and to have the players presented to them on the field. The third week of the month, after an Investiture, a luncheon party, and an audience for the Prime Minister, besides many lesser engagements, was marked by a visit to the borough and university of Reading; and on the 28th a strenuous day in the North Midlands took in visits to Repton School, the City of Derby, the Needwood Estate of the Duchy of Lancaster, and the town of Burton-on-Trent.

The peculiar institution of the Duchy of Lancaster perhaps requires here a word of historical explanation. In the fourteenth century the earls and dukes of Lancaster, by judicious marriages with other great families and eventually with the Royal House, built up a chain of earldoms stretching right across England from the Mersey to the Wash and became so powerful as to be able to overawe the King himself. Eventually Henry of Bolingbroke, Duke of Lancaster, dispossessed his cousin Richard II and seized the throne as Henry IV. As King he bestowed the dukedom of Lancaster on his eldest son, Henry of Monmouth; but when that son in turn acceded in 1413 as King Henry V he judged that the dukedom was too formidable a possession to be entrusted to any subject. It has never since been regranted; but by the settlement made in the fifteenth century the lands of the duchy are constituted a private inheritance for the Sovereign personally, to be kept for ever separate from the national revenue and to provide an income for his support.

In the duchy itself it is customary to refer to the reigning monarch as the Duke (even when she is a woman) of Lancaster; but this is only a pleasant and pious observance, with no validity in law. Legally, every peerage whose holder accedes to the Throne "merges" in the Crown until it is regranted, and Lancaster is no exception to the rule; so that the Queen is no more (and no less) Duke of Lancaster than she is Duke or Duchess of York or Clarence, or Countess of Mortain, to name a few of the dignities held by some of her predecessors before their accession. But on the Duchy estates she appears as the landowner rather than the Sovereign, and is faithful to the tradition of her ancestors in taking a close personal interest in the welfare of her tenants.

April began with a good deal of state and ceremonial business— two meetings of the Privy Council in the first week, an audience for the Prime Minister, two presentation parties for debutantes, and a number of lesser engagements; there was even an audience for the Chancellor of the Exchequer in connexion with his Budget on Sunday the seventh, because the Queen was about to leave the country. Nevertheless time was found at the week-end for the Queen and the Duke of Edinburgh to attend the 350th anniversary of the elevation of Romsey to the rank of a borough— though of course as the seat of a great medieval abbey it is many centuries older.

The second week of April was occupied with a state visit to France, and the third was Holy Week, during which the Queen, in honour of the centenary celebrations at St. Alban's

Abbey Church, transferred the annual ceremony of the royal Maundy there from its usual scene in Westminster Abbey. From there she went as usual at Easter to Windsor; but in Easter week itself she and the Duke paid the two-day visit to Worcestershire and Herefordshire which has already been described in detail. At the end of the week she was back at the Castle to review the annual parade of the Queen's Scouts, postponed to Low Sunday from St. George's Day. After holding a Council and receiving the Prime Minister on the Monday, she moved to Sandringham on Tuesday, the last day of the month, leaving the Duke of Edinburgh to make Windsor his base for a few visits to service institutions.

They were both back at Buckingham Palace on Friday, May 3, in time for the Queen to pay a visit to the Royal Naval College, Greenwich, on the Saturday morning, and for both to attend the Football Association's Cup Final at Wembley in the afternoon. As usual the players were presented, and the winners received the cup from the hands of the Queen. After this there was a fortnight crowded with political and diplomatic engagements, which kept the Queen closely tied to Buckingham Palace until May 18, when she left London by train for Hull, to embark there in the Royal Yacht for a state visit to Denmark. On the way home she and the Duke of Edinburgh spent two days at Invergordon with the Home Fleet, which had sailed out into the North Sea to meet them, and now took pride and pleasure in showing their Sovereign over some of her greatest ships. She left the *Britannia* on Wednesday, May 29, at Lossiemouth, and put herself in the hands of her Royal Naval Air Service to be flown back to London in time to receive the Prime Minister on the last day of the month.

However, after a week-end with the children at Sandringham, both the Queen and the Duke of Edinburgh were back in Scotland on Tuesday, June 4, to inspect the R.A.F. Station of Fighter Command at Leuchars; but this was very much a flying visit, for the Prime Minister was due at Buckingham Palace for his weekly audience at half-past six that evening. On Friday she was at the Queen Elizabeth Hospital for Children at Banstead in Surrey, and after the Whitsun week-end attended the opening of the Royal Tournament, the joint display of the prowess of all her three fighting services, at Earls Court, Kensington. Next day, Thursday, June 13, was the official celebration of her birthday, and she took the salute at the traditional ceremony of Trooping the Colour on the Horse Guards Parade. On the fourteenth, with her consort, she was doing honour to the art of the greatest English poet at the Shakespeare Memorial Theatre, Stratford-on-Avon.

The third week of June, according to custom, was spent at Windsor Castle. It opened with the splendid and historic annual ceremonies of the Order of the Garter, including the investiture and installation of two new knights—Lord Ismay and Lord Middleton—and the procession through the wards of the Castle for the solemn service of thanksgiving in St. George's Chapel. The rest of the week was an occasion for the Queen's private hospitality in her country home, at which as usual the principal entertainment offered to her distinguished guests was daily attendance at Ascot Races. The Sovereigns of England in semi-state have been accustomed for generations to preside over this famous event, as the principal symbol of the patronage they give to the great national industry of bloodstock breeding. It is both a popular spectacle and the outstanding annual concourse of the fashionable world, so that there is no doubt that the Queen's presence, and the brilliance of her drive down the course, give immense pleasure to all classes of her subjects. It is an occasion both for elegant display and for mass junketings; and the stern consciences that disapprove of both these things will always maintain that the Queen is wasting her time at Ascot. Others, more numerous, who think that bright colours and the joy of life are an indispensable element in the expression of a nation's character will think it a fully representative and queenly act to give the royal blessing to this sparkling festival. The fact that racing happens to be the favourite amusement of the Queen herself detracts nothing from the merit of the office she there performs. "What great cause is he identified with?" asks the disgruntled opponent when Arnold Bennett's "the Card" is elected mayor; and the answer is "He's identified with the great cause of cheering us all up".

Another national sport should have been honoured by the Queen on Monday, June 24; but the test match with the West Indies had ended prematurely on the Saturday, so she could not carry out her plan of going to Lord's. Instead, the West Indian team were invited to meet her at Buckingham Palace—one of seven engagements there on that day, apart from a meeting of the Privy Council, so that possibly it was something of a relief that there was no cricket. There were even more numerous functions the following day, but somehow time was contrived to go to Greenwich and open to the public the famous clipper *Cutty Sark*, which had come there to its last anchorage. On Wednesday the Queen entertained the Prime Ministers of the Commonwealth to dinner, and on Friday the members of their staffs, who were assembled for one of their periodic conferences in London; and on the intervening day she and the Duke of Edinburgh paid a visit to Guildford. So June ended and the year was half-way through.

July opened with an easy week: the only engagements outside the Palace were at the Royal Agricultural Society's show at Norwich and the finals of the lawn tennis championships at Wimbledon. The next week, after a visit to the Union Jack services club in the Waterloo Road, in South London, the Queen and the Duke made a rapid dash north, first to Yorkshire, where they saw the York mystery plays, toured the Great Yorkshire Show at Harrogate, and inspected several mechanized cavalry regiments at Catterick Camp; and then to the city of Chester and the Wirral Peninsula. This was all accomplished in two days, Wednesday and Thursday, allowing the Queen to receive official callers at Buckingham Palace as usual on the Friday morning. For the next fortnight ceremonial duties kept her in London, for there were two investitures of persons included in the Birthday Honours List, and the two summer garden parties at Buckingham Palace, at each of which some 7,000 of her subjects were entertained. It was not until Wednesday, July 24 that the Queen and the Duke could leave Southampton in the Royal Yacht, in order to receive the loyal acclamation of the people of the four islands of Jersey, Guernsey, Sark and Alderney, where she reigns under the ancient title of Duchess of Normandy. Returning to Portsmouth on Saturday, July 27, she welcomed the members of the American Bar Association at a garden party on the following Monday, attended the Boy Scouts' Jamboree at Sutton Coldfield on the Saturday, visited the Girl Guides in camp at Windsor on Sunday, and at last left London in the royal train for Balmoral on Wednesday, August 7.

This summer holiday was broken in September, when the Queen and the Duke came south for two days to take their son to school, but ended on October 8, when her "winter term" opened with a Privy Council at Buckingham Palace, followed by an audience for the Prime Minister the following day. The two remaining days of that week were closely packed with "home" engagements; and on Saturday, October 12, the Queen and the Duke of Edinburgh flew off on their ten-day visit to Canada and the United States. So the new season for outside functions in the United Kingdom more properly began with a visit to Brentwood and the new town of Harlow on October 30. The Queen had to be back at Buckingham Palace the next day to give luncheon to the President of Pakistan, and in the afternoon to hold a Council and receive the Prime Minister.

The Royal Film Performance, the annual event by which the Queen shows her representative interest in one of the youngest and most popular of the arts, was given on Monday, November 4; and on Tuesday she drove in the Irish State Coach to the Palace of Westminster to open Parliament in state with the Speech from the Throne, outlining the Government's programme for the new session.

Next day the Queen visited Goodenough House, an establishment of the Sister Trust, and London House, which is a hall of residence for students of all races of the Commonwealth studying in London, whether in the university (of which the Queen Mother is Chancellor) or any other of the teaching institutions of the capital. These were short afternoon forays from Buckingham Palace, and did not prevent her discharging several important engagements within her own walls, including the reception of the Sultan of Brunei. The numerous official visitors in the rest of the week included on the Saturday the wife of the Chairman of the British Legion, who came to sell poppies to the Queen and all the members and servants of the Household, and on the Sunday, according to custom, the Queen stood at the head of her people before the Cenotaph in Whitehall and laid her wreath of poppies at its foot, in commemoration of the dead of the Commonwealth and Empire in two world wars.

For the rest of November nearly all the Queen's engagements were within the Palace: they included a Privy Council, several investitures, a presentation party for members of the diplomatic corps, and a luncheon to Prince Rainier and Princess Grace of Monaco. The Grand Duke of Luxembourg also came to tea, with Princess Josephine Charlotte. In December, a month in which political and diplomatic engagements heavily predominate, the Queen paid a compliment to the newspaper Press by spending an evening in Printing House Square, where she watched the whole complex and lengthy process of setting up and printing *The Times* for the following day. She was moving in a related atmosphere a few days later when she attended the rededication service of the Church of St. Bride's, Fleet Street, restored to the beauty of Wren's exquisite design after heavy damage by German incendiary bombs; for this is traditionally the church of the newspaper profession. But it was also an international occasion, for the Queen unveiled a monument of Anglo-American friendship in the form of a new reredos, presented to the church in memory of Edward Winslow, Governor of Massachusetts in the days of the Pilgrim Fathers. The staff dance at Buckingham Palace, and the distribution of Christmas presents to the Household and servants, filled the interstices between official engagements in the few days intervening before the Queen left, with her family, on December 21, for Sandringham there to complete her year's programme of social intercourse with her subjects by broadcasting her message of greeting and goodwill to all of them, round the five continents and the seven seas, on the afternoon of Christmas Day.

Work of State and Government

Work of State and Government

THE foregoing chapters have by deliberate intent avoided any but incidental treatment of the function of the Queen as the political head and formal ruler of her kingdoms. That, as has been repeatedly emphasized, is only one aspect of her all-embracing representation of her peoples: she is the head of society in all its diverse manifestations, and in one of those manifestations we call it the State. Nevertheless it is fundamental to the British way of life to believe that a man is not fully civilized and free unless he has some share in the government of the community to which he belongs. Government is concerned with the conditions of the good life, and is therefore important to all rational beings; correspondingly, the part that the Queen plays in assisting government, and especially self-government, is important too.

The Queen's original contribution to government is that she, over the whole of its range, communicates the impulse that sets its machinery in motion. She is the head of all its interlocked departments—the legislature, the executive, the judiciary. Parliament cannot meet save on her summons; no military or civilian official can give an order save under authority that in the last resort is delegated by her; the judges who interpret the law require to be appointed by the Queen.

In order that the solemn and indeed sacred significance of the governance of men may be kept vividly before the imagination of the people, the Queen is on certain occasions invested with very great visible splendour and majesty. The chief of these occasions are specially associated with her initiating function: when she is opening her reign, or when she is opening the cycle of the parliamentary year, she is displayed in her most transcendent glory—not vainglory, not for her personal gratification, but in order that she may hold up before the eyes of the people an image of their grandest traditions and their most exalted hopes.

The greatest of all royal ceremonials, and the most full of profound meaning, is the high solemnity of the Coronation. The complexity of modern organization, the vast number of people all round the Commonwealth and Empire who need to be consulted and make their own arrangements, have a little obscured its ancient significance as a renewal of the national life at the very outset of a new reign; where it was once celebrated immediately after the funeral of the late Sovereign, it is now postponed for more than a year after the accession. Nevertheless at the coronation of Queen Elizabeth II, made visible far and wide, as no previous coronation could be, by the progress of scientific invention, the patriotic imagination of the multitudes was undoubtedly sufficient to supply the defects of the calendar, and experience the uplifting of the heart with a sense of a fresh start and a fresh dedication.

The colour and pageantry of that famous day are fresh in memory, and have been many times described by more eloquent pens than can be brought to bear upon these pages. But it will be appropriate here to consider the symbolic significance of the ceremony, for its illumination of the place of the monarchy in the national and imperial life.

The rite of coronation has developed slowly over many centuries, and each phase of history has left its mark upon it; so that to-day it stands as an epitome of an immemorial tradition. In order to understand it fully, it is necessary to go very far back.

Especially the rite embodies the memory of the conversion of pagan England to Christianity. In the most primitive form we can trace for the inauguration of a new reign, the King took his seat on a ceremonial stone—which may once have been the tomb of his predecessor, with whose spirit he thus established communion; and having thus been installed he feasted at a great banquet with all the great men of the realm.

These simple elements survived at the heart of the coronation ceremony until the nineteenth century; in a mutilated form they survive still. From the Norman Conquest until 1831 the day began with the placing of the new King by the peers of the realm in a stone chair placed on the "King's Bench" in Westminster Hall—his symbolic seat of government; and they ended with a banquet, itself encrusted with symbolism, in the same famous building. But in between these two phases of the pagan inauguration there arrived a procession of clergy from the Abbey Church across the road, bringing with them the Crown and other emblems of Christian kingship, and inviting the King to come with them to seek the blessing of God before proceeding to the creature pleasures of the feast. Thereupon the clergy and the secular lords combined to escort the King to the Abbey, the Crown being borne aloft in full view of the crowds in the streets. But the vast and vulgar ostentation with which George IV chose to celebrate his coronation banquet in 1831 caused such a revulsion towards cheese-paring economy that the whole of the proceedings in Westminster Hall were suspended by his successor, William IV, and have never been resumed.

Precedents have accumulated against history. In 1952 the pleading of scholars who understood the significance of the ancient forms for a resumption of the full and balanced ritual was frustrated once more by the inertia of officials. Most ironically, they were accused of wishing to do violence to tradition, since the bureaucratic mind talks glibly of immemorial custom when it means no more than "what we did last time". So in place of the gathering of the magnates in Westminster Hall an expensive and unnecessary annexe is built to disfigure the western approach to the Abbey, where the Crown and insignia are laid out beyond sight of the people, and to which the Westminster clergy, singing the litany, come down to meet the Queen, also unseen by any but the privileged few. This tattered fragment of the ancient custom still clings about the religious rite, but in such an attenuated form that only a few specialists understand what is going on. The rite itself, however, was carefully revised for Queen Elizabeth II, and the changes made tended to undo the bungled work of recent centuries and bring out more clearly its true significance.

According to the mediaeval ritual books, the King should spend the night before the coronation in prayer. For all that can here be said to the contrary, Queen Elizabeth may have done the like; certainly the sense of spiritual exaltation that radiated from her was almost tangible to those of us who stood near her in the Abbey. But in the more mundane sense also she had undergone a long and strenuous preparation for the event. The frequent and detailed private rehearsals of every movement of her own part constituted only a small fraction of this preparation. For weeks beforehand there had been subsidiary functions and ceremonies, and men and women of mark were crowding into London from all parts of the Commonwealth and beyond, including members of all the royal families of the world and exalted representatives from all the republics, not excepting Soviet Russia. Royal hospitality had to be shown to all these eminences, and innumerable audiences given to personages with public business to discuss. The red boxes multiplied; and the always crowded engagement book at Buckingham Palace, parts of which have been analysed for normal times in earlier chapters, were now packed to the point of physical exhaustion.

So when the psalm "I was glad when they said unto me, We will go into the house of the Lord" hailed the Queen's entry into Westminster Abbey, the moment was only a climax reached by a long and laborious approach. She was preceded by secular lords carrying the various objects of the regalia, who now surrendered these emblems, the Crown among them, to the Archbishop of Canterbury to be laid upon the altar, in token of the submission of worldly authority to God.

The first act to be performed was the presentation of the Queen to the people. If the preliminary enthronement in Westminster Hall had been carried out, the meaning of this would have been enhanced. For then the Queen would have come to the Abbey conspicuously as the choice of Parliament, which has inherited the authority of the mediaeval lords who raised her ancestors to the stone chair on the King's Bench. She does in fact, as is well known, hold her office by a parliamentary title—under the Act of Settlement, 1701, which secures the Throne to the heirs general of the Electress Sophia, conditionally on their being Protestants. So far as any recognition in the ceremony went, this nomination by Act of Parliament had to be taken on trust when the Archbishop, traditionally the first subject and therefore the champion of popular liberties, showed the Queen to the congregation and asked them to declare the people's approval of the choice and "signify their willingness and joy" by loud and repeated acclamations of "God save Queen Elizabeth". The actual acclamations were left to the Queen's Scholars of Westminster School, who by ancient custom have the privilege of being the voice of the people on this occasion.

Now the Queen could be deemed to have been presented by Parliament and people for the blessing of the Church; the Church, however, does not bless indiscriminately, but requires first to be satisfied of the good intentions of the postulant. The Archbishop therefore asked the Queen to swear a threefold oath, to govern each of her sovereign peoples according to its own laws, to cause law and justice, with mercy, to be executed in all her judgments, and to maintain in the United Kingdom the Protestant Reformed religion established by law.

The coronation oath has a continuous history going back at least to A.D. 973. In a sense the whole constitutional theory of limited monarchy has developed out of it: Magna Charta, for example, has been regarded as simply an elaborate expansion of the coronation oath taken by the Angevin kings. Its placing as a preliminary to the whole coronation—the only stage at which the Queen's own voice was heard—was an emphatic assertion that the authority of the Queen is strictly subject to the law; and therefore that all authority is similarly subject, for all authority is deemed to be delegated in the last resort from the Queen. Immediately after swearing, by a new rearrangement of the rite, she was presented with the Bible, as "the rule for the whole life and government of Christian Princes"; did she perhaps remember how in her broadcast at her coming of age, immediately after vowing to devote her whole life to the service of the people, she had prayed that God would help her to make good her vow?

The recognition and the oath were only a prelude to the great act of consecration. The coronation proper was inserted in a long interlude in the communion service, primarily in order to invest it with the greatest possible sanctity, but also with the effect of emphasizing that everything done to her or by her in the rite was to be understood as having relation to the peoples of whom she is the representative: for communion is by definition an act, the quintessential act, of communal fellowship and brotherhood.

When the appropriate moment came, at the end of the creed, the Queen was divested of all the gorgeous robes in which she had made her entrance, and clothed only in the simplest possible white garment—in token at once of the humility and innocency with which earthly power must present itself before God—took her seat in the coronation chair of King Edward I. (This is the chair that holds in its base the legendary Stone of Scone, supposed to have been Jacob's pillow at Bethel, on which the ancient Kings of Scots were crowned.) Here the Archbishop anointed her on the hands, the breast and the head, with consecrated oil, "as kings, priests and prophets were anointed, and as Solomon was anointed king by Zadok the priest and Nathan the prophet". This was the moment of supreme spiritual import in the rite;

for the unction, originally no doubt a symbolic act of purification, was anciently regarded as miraculously conveying the mysterious quality that sets kings apart from common humanity. "Not all the water in the rude rough sea," says Shakespeare's Richard II, "can wash the balm from an anointed king". According to the older usage, it is only at this point of the ceremony that the ritual would have given her the title of Queen: till then she would be referred to simply as the Duchess (of Normandy, Aquitaine, or in her individual case Edinburgh).

Now that the anointed Princess had become fully a Queen in the sight of God, the time had come to give her the elaborate garments and emblems which only the Lord's Anointed may wear or hold. One of these is the Crown, but there are many others, each with its own symbolical meaning. One after the other she received the sword, symbolic of justice and defence, which she immediately offered up to God on the altar; the bracelets standing for the divine protection, the imperial robe of righteousness, the orb with the cross above it, declaring that the whole earth is subject to the power of Christ, the ring, regarded at least from the time of Elizabeth I as the wedding ring uniting her to her country, and then the sceptre, which is the oldest of all symbols of royal authority. No doubt its remotest archetype is the branch that the first man or pre-man pulled down from a tree to enable him to impose his will upon his fellows. It is the ultimate representation of power. But two things of profound significance are to be noted about its treatment in the English coronation service. First, as the sceptre of authority was placed in the Queen's right hand the rod with the dove was simultaneously put into her left, to show that the exercise of the power of law is always to be tempered with mercy. Secondly, although the sceptre stands for the plenitude of authority, its bestowal in the investiture is made subordinate to that of the proudest symbol of all, the Crown of St. Edward; and in setting this upon the Queen's head the Archbishop said no word about power, speaking only of glory and righteousness, faith and good works. So in the heart of the coronation ritual itself there is embodied the innermost secret of the British monarchy as a way of life— the recognition that power is not the highest of earthly attributes, and that the Queen exists to keep it in its proper subordination to the totality of the people's life, for which she stands.

Having thus been invested with all the symbolic attributes of royalty, Elizabeth II, anointed, sceptred and crowned, was fully and visibly a Queen, but not yet of any determinate realm. The last act of the coronation, therefore, was to lead her from King Edward's chair and place her in the Throne, by which parable she was given formal possession of the Kingdom of England; after which, in their several ranks, her bishops and lay lords—beginning with her husband—knelt to do her fealty or homage. Thus the oath of good government, by which the Queen had pledged herself to her people at the outset of the ceremony, was answered by the oath of loyal service tendered to her by the heads of the people at the end.

This great solemnity of the coronation, then, is far more than a splendid spectacle; and indeed its spectacular side, noble and moving as it is, has here been wholly ignored. Rather is it a superb ritual drama, a wonderful allegory of the relation of God and man, of society and the individual, of Church and State, of power and life. Intimately as the exultation of it all is involved with its venerable antiquity and the continuity of the national growth for which it stands, there are several respects in which, without doing violence to tradition, it could be, and ought to be, better adjusted to the contemporary world.

Most notably, there was scarcely any allusion in the ceremony of 1953 to the fact that Elizabeth II was Queen of seven distinct and sovereign realms, and head of a worldwide Commonwealth in which still other nations, not themselves monarchies, were included. For historical reasons, indeed, she was crowned not even as Queen of the United Kingdom, but of England alone—

Scotland having been content since the Act of Union to recognize as its sovereign the person crowned at Westminster. In this essential nature, indeed, the coronation could probably not be modified, for it is a quasi-sacrament of the Church of England, and it is only in England that this Church is established. But much more might have been done to surround the Queen in the Abbey with great personages representative of the whole of her Commonwealth, and to give them a symbolic part to play at least in the secular ceremonies surrounding the inner rite, such as the swearing of homage or the preliminary enthronement in Westminster Hall, if that ancient scene had been included.

If in making room near the Queen's person for eminent statesmen from her realms oversea it had been necessary to curtail the space allotted to the swollen ranks of the English peerage, that would have been a small price to pay for making the company about her throne more realistically representative of the living social order. These matters will need to be considered before another coronation is celebrated—very many years hence, as we confidently hope. They do not affect the spiritual worth of the solemnity of June 2, 1953, in which the Queen enacted on behalf of her people the high and ancient drama of national dedication and benediction.

The state opening of Parliament is in origin a kind of annual echo of the coronation. Three times in the year the Norman kings of England were accustomed to "wear their crowns" ceremonially—at Gloucester on Christmas Day, at Winchester for Easter, and in Westminster at Pentecost. On these occasions the great men of the realm were summoned to attend, and out of their meetings Parliament gradually developed. The mark of this origin remains, in that the first meeting of a new session of Parliament is as much a social as a political occasion.

It is also the principal occasion of the year for holding up the monarchy in its full glory before the eyes of the people. The

133

Queen drives in state from Buckingham Palace in the Irish State Coach—a remarkable eighteenth-century equipage with elaborately painted panels, whose ancient timbers give continual cause for anxiety, but which seems to have a few years of life in it still. It is usually drawn by that famous team of horses, the Windsor Greys. In his magnificent uniform of scarlet and gold lace, the Master of the Horse, one of the three great officers of the Household, rides at the carriage wheel, ready to receive the Sovereign's commands. She herself is dressed in white, with a diamond tiara of crosses formy and fleurs de lys on her head and the blue riband of the Order of the Garter crossing diagonally from her left shoulder; the same emblem adorns the Duke of Edinburgh, in the full dress of an admiral of the fleet at her side. The processional way along the Mall and Whitehall is lined by the regiments of Foot Guards; a Sovereign's Escort of the Household Cavalry, with plumes and cuirasses and bearing the Standard, rides in front and behind the coach. So the people are shown the simple woman, who at other times can move among them so familiarly, exalted into a hieratic symbol of all their national glory and greatness. The fusion of the simplicity into the grandeur is a parable of the way of life called monarchy—which is a mystery, but a mystery by which a people live.

Meanwhile, inside the Houses of Parliament, another parable is being prepared. From at least the fifteenth century it has been the teaching of the doctors of the constitution that the fullest majesty and authority of kingship is attained only when the King, or Queen, is surrounded by the three Estates of the Realm in full Parliament assembled. The meaning of that familiar word "parliament" needs a little consideration. The range of buildings in which the ceremony takes place is properly known as the Palace of Westminster. It was founded by King Edward the Confessor to be the principal home of the Kings and Queens of England. They have long since placed it on almost permanent

loan to their subjects for the business of representative government; but on this one day of the year the Queen resumes possession of her official home in order to give a house-warming party.
The guests are the principal men and women of the realm; they
have received invitations, called "writs of summons", sent out
by her Lord Chancellor, who is the original private secretary
of the Sovereign grown to huge proportions. He signs them
on her behalf with the Great Seal of England—"seal" is the
Latin "sigillum", the diminutive of "signum"; signing by
"subscription", or writing the name at the foot, is a comparatively modern substitute for this more formal signature.

The guests are invited first and foremost as an act of friendship
and courtesy by their hostess; but the occasion is to be taken to
hold a "parley" with them on the public affairs of the kingdom
in which she and they are partners; so they are asked to meet her
in the "parlour" of her Palace, which has the necessary amenities
for such comprehensive talk. As the parley is a very great parley,
its homely name is expanded into the more imposing "parliament"; and similarly the parlour where it takes place is magnified
into the Parliament Chamber: it is the room generally known as
the House of Lords.

The hostess's seat, called the Throne, is set under a canopy at
one end of the great apartment, with an armchair for the Duke
of Edinburgh at a lower level on its left. This, by the way, is
the Throne proper; all other thrones, for example in the state
apartments at Buckingham Palace or even in Westminster Abbey
for the coronation, are but local substitutes for it. On either side,
arrayed in their party dresses, or parliamentary robes of scarlet
trimmed with minever according to their degree, are the
members of the House of Lords, on this one occasion sitting in
strict order of precedence.

In earlier times, when the proportions of the First and Second
Estates were approximately even, the whole of the right side
would be occupied by the Lords Spiritual, with the Archbishop

of Canterbury nearest the Throne and the junior bishop farthest away, and the left by the Lords Temporal, tailing away from dukes through marquesses, earls and viscounts to the common run of barons. But now the secular ranks are so swollen that the lay peers of the lesser degrees overflow from the far end of their own benches on to the cross benches and so up what should be the spiritual side, so that the junior barons link up with the little group of bishops, who are only twenty-six strong even if all are present. But still the Archbishop of Canterbury as head of the First Estate faces across the gangway to the Duke of Gloucester as head of the Second.

This, however, is a party first and a political event second; and so quite a number of people are present merely as the Queen's guests and not as politicians at all. So far as there is room the peers are permitted to bring their wives, who in evening dress with tiaras occupy a number of benches interspersed between those of the legislators. The judges are there, in their full-bottomed wigs and ermine or gold-embroidered robes, sitting in a huddle on the woolsacks; and so are the Queen's personal lawyers, known at ordinary times as the Attorney and Solicitor General. And finally a number of distinguished foreigners, representatives of her brother and sister sovereigns (which "sovereigns" nowadays are as often as not republican governments) have been bidden: a large box is set aside for the diplomatic corps on the right of the Throne.

As the Queen leaves her coach at the Norman Porch she is received by the Lord Great Chamberlain, the keeper of her Palace of Westminster, and the Earl Marshal, the director of royal ceremonies; and with these two Great Officers of State walking backwards before her she ascends the stairs, which are lined by the heralds in their armorial tabards, to the Robing Room, where she is invested with her parliament robe with its long train of crimson velvet and with the Imperial State Crown, which has been brought from the Tower of London under cavalry escort in advance. She despatches the Gentleman Usher of the Black Rod, a servant of the Order of the Garter who is generally seconded to attend the House of Lords, to bid the Speaker and Members of the House of Commons to meet her in the Parliament Chamber. Close on his heels she herself leaves the Robing Room and, preceded by the heralds and closely attended by the Great Officers of State and her household dignitaries, walks in procession through the Royal Gallery, where some hundreds of privileged spectators are assembled to see her pass. Her hand is held high by the Duke of Edinburgh; her train is carried by two pages in scarlet coats of eighteenth-century cut; her ladies-in-waiting and the Mistress of the Robes walk behind. The Yeomen of the Guard are posted on either side of the Gallery; the Gentlemen at Arms, with ceremonial axes and tall plumed helmets, are drawn up in the Prince's chamber, which is the anteroom of the House of Lords.

As the Queen enters, the lights, which have been lowered, flash up and are reflected from diamonds and gold all round the assembly. The Duke of Edinburgh hands the Queen to her Throne, and two peers take post on either side of her, one holding upright the sheathed Sword of State—the same that was bestowed upon her at the coronation—the other bearing the Cap of Maintenance, an object of doubtful significance, which possibly represents the long-lost duchy of Aquitaine. "My lords," says the Queen, "pray be seated." There is a short pause, while the Commons, arriving in procession two by two behind their Speaker, take their ancient places, standing at the Bar of the House. Once more the possessors of real power are required to make symbolic gestures of humility in the presence of the people's supreme representative, the Queen, who stands for so much greater things than power alone. Then the Lord Chancellor, on his knees before the Throne, takes from the emblazoned Purse that should contain the Great Seal a sheet of printed paper, and hands it to the Queen.

This is the Gracious Speech opening the Session of Parliament, which, remaining seated, she proceeds to read to the assembly. It is of necessity a prosaic document, in curious contrast with the glamorous setting in which it is read. The Queen has seen it a day or two before, and has given her formal approval to its contents; but she has had nothing to do with its composition. It is simply a programme of the business that the Cabinet proposes to set before Parliament in the coming session; and though each House will shortly adjourn to move stately addresses of gratitude in reply to Her Majesty's Most Gracious Speech, the debates on these addresses, lasting several days, will contain no reference to the Queen, but consist entirely of attack and defence of the party Government in office, covering the whole range of its declared policy and any omissions that the Opposition may claim to have detected. Such is the convention of the constitution, which regards Ministers as the Queen's servants, while holding the Queen as a person entirely detached from the party battle which fills their parliamentary life.

At the end of the Speech the procession re-forms, and departs very much as it came. There has been a splendid spectacle, steeped in history and full of significant allusion for all who seek to understand the meaning of parliamentary self-government. In it the Queen has played the greatest ceremonial part which, outside the coronation, she is ever called upon to perform. Hitherto, however, she has been seen performing it only by her fellow-actors in the drama and a minute proportion of the millions whom parliamentary self-government concerns. This year, after many doubts and hesitations, the decision has been taken to display this intensely significant ritual to the multitudes by means of television. There were many who thought that television of the actual reading of the Speech from the Throne might be held to injure the valuable intimacy of Parliament and impose an unfair strain on the Queen herself. It has also been objected that the Speech would be misunderstood by the masses as an expression of the Queen's personal involvement in party politics; but this argument seems to take an unnecessarily low view of the people's understanding of the constitution under which they live. The detachment of the Queen from party politics must not be exaggerated beyond bounds. She is, after all, officially identified with the views of the party commanding a majority of the House of Commons, for so long as the House is willing to bestow its confidence. Nevertheless, the televising of the State Opening is only an experiment, and judgment has yet to be passed on its results.

Having with this ancient ceremony set the business of Parliament in motion, the Queen is not seen again in the Palace of Westminster for the remainder of the session. The pleasant habit of Queen Anne, who used to sit in an armchair by the fire, theoretically invisible, to listen to the debates of the House of Lords, has long ago been abandoned: the new Victorian-Gothic House of Lords was rebuilt without a fireplace. The Queen does not even, as is popularly supposed, "sign" Acts of Parliament. What happens is that at the end of the session, or earlier if enough Bills have accumulated that need to be brought into force quickly, a number of peers, generally three, are appointed Lords Commissioners to give the Royal Assent.

These Commissioners, putting on their parliamentary robes and cocked hats, take their seats in front of the Throne in the House of Lords, and Black Rod is dispatched to summon the Commons to the Bar. The Commons, having first slammed their door in the face of Black Rod, to assert their privilege of denying him admittance if they feel so disposed, open it again to his knock, and interrupt their debate to hear his message, which he delivers with bows and compliments, desiring the attendance of this Honourable House to hear the Royal Assent given to certain measures. Headed by the Speaker, a reasonable number of Members then walk in pairs across the Central Lobby to the Bar of the House of Lords. When they have arrived, the Clerk of the Parliaments, at the table in the middle of the House, reads the titles of the Bills that have passed both Houses, and to each ordinary Bill the senior of the Lords Commissioners pronounces the words "La Reyne le veult"—preserving for this formal occasion the Norman French which was still the language of the governing classes, and therefore of Parliament, when the procedure of legislation by Bill took shape in the fourteenth century. If the Bill is the annual Finance Bill, or any other measure imposing taxation, there is a longer formula to the effect that the Queen thanks her good subjects, accepts their benevolence, and so wills it to be.

Could the Queen refuse her Royal Assent? In any personal sense she certainly could not. This final stage of the making of law is one of the most solemn acts ever done in the name of a constitutional monarch, even if she does not choose to be physically present on the Throne to see it done; and therefore she must perform it strictly on the advice of her Ministers responsible to Parliament. And it is in the highest degree improbable that her Ministers would ever advise her to say "no". For if the measure had been carried through the House of Commons against their express opposition, they would by constitutional custom have the choice only between resigning, to be replaced by a new Ministry presumably in favour of the Bill, or advising the Queen to dissolve Parliament before the Bill could reach the stage at which the Royal Assent was asked for. It is not surprising therefore that there has been no example of the refusal of Assent since the modern Cabinet system began to take shape in the reign of Queen Anne.

Nevertheless, the giving of the Royal Assent is a formality that cannot be dispensed with, and circumstances are perhaps imaginable in which Ministers might advise the Queen to withhold it. For example, there may have been a sudden change of Government, without dissolution of Parliament, while some controversial measure which had passed both Houses was waiting for the final act that would make it into law. Even so, the

Cabinet that advised this method of disposing of it, instead of allowing it to pass and then asking Parliament to repeal it, would have to be exceedingly sure of its ground, and absolutely confident of such overwhelming support that it need not fear that the Commons, a very touchy body, would take offence.

But suppose that in the great "gold standard" crisis of 1931, when Mr. Ramsay MacDonald resigned as Labour Prime Minister and was persuaded by King George V to resume office as head of a Coalition—suppose that at that very moment Lords Commissioners were about to pronounce the King's assent to one of those measures of heavy expenditure which the May Commission had just reported were leading the country to imminent bankruptcy. That might have been an occasion for the new Government to advise the King not to let his Commissioners give the Royal Assent.

A similar situation might conceivably arise, without a change of Government, through unforeseen foreign action. A Bill might just have passed the House of Lords authorizing the supply of nuclear bombs to Barataria, with which the Foreign Office was trying to conclude an alliance; and then Barataria might startle the world—as Russia did with the Molotov-Ribbentrop pact of August 1939—by announcing that she had entered into a military compact with our arch-enemy, Ruritania. No one would then be likely to attack the Government if, when the Clerk of the Parliaments read out the title of the Barataria (Nuclear Armament Aid) Bill, the Lords Commissioners replied with the phrase that has not been heard for two and a half centuries, "La Reyne s'avisera"—"the Queen will think it over". (The Kings and Queens of England never say "no" to their loyal subjects; but after those words have been spoken nothing more is heard of the Bill.)

The giving or conceivably withholding of the Royal Assent to parliamentary Bills is then an action in which the Queen participates, so to speak, at second hand, through her Lords

Commissioners—whom she also employs, again as advised by her Ministers, to convey to Parliament her order of prorogation, which closes the session. But the Assent is nevertheless hers, because it is she who appoints the Commissioners and gives them their instructions. How does she do this? It is one of the very large number of royal actions which are performed by "the Queen in Council".

Just as legislation is passed by "the Queen in Parliament" and the source of all justice is "the Queen on the Bench", so the supreme executive power, the power, that is, to apply and enforce the law that Parliament has made and the Courts interpreted, resides in "the Queen in Council". The Privy Council is in a sense the residual form of the original undifferentiated governing body of Norman England, of which Parliament is an occasional expansion and the courts of law a delegation.

To-day it is a company of two or three hundred persons, of whom the nucleus are statesmen who hold or have held high government office, but which also includes the archbishops and senior bishops, the higher judges, and some men and women of outstanding eminence who are appointed to the Council as a personal honour. It is also usual to appoint the Prime Ministers and occasionally some of their most distinguished colleagues from the Queen's realms oversea, though the functions of the Privy Council are in the main limited to the United Kingdom and the normal place of these statesmen is in the corresponding Executive Councils of the Governors-General whom they advise.

There are a number of committees of the Privy Council, of which by far the most important is that which we call the Cabinet. No one can sit in the Cabinet without first being "sworn of the Council"; and the oath that he then takes to preserve the Queen's secrets is the basis of the confidential character of Cabinet proceedings. As a Privy Councillor a Minister has the constitutional right to "advise" the Queen, and bears the responsibility in Parliament for what she does on the advice that he gives. Some of the things that his department does under his direction are required by law to be authorized by the Queen in Council; and this means that the Council must physically assemble, and the Queen in her own person agree to what is being done in her name. It may be almost anything, from a declaration of war to a change in the purchase tax on toy soldiers: if the relevant statute says that a power is given to the Queen in Council, then the Queen and her councillors must meet before it can be lawfully exercised.

"Her councillors", however, does not mean the whole three hundred of them. Although membership of the Council is for life, constitutional convention ordains that only those councillors who are in agreement with the Queen's ministerial advisers for the time being shall be active in its work. A senior member of the Government is appointed by the Queen, on the Prime Minister's advice, Lord President of the Council: so stereotyped is the convention that it is not unusual for the position to be combined with the headship of the party organization, as it now is by Lord Hailsham.

At any meeting of the Council only those councillors attend who are summoned by the Clerk of the Council on the Lord President's instructions. The rest not only do not attend; they would not be admitted even if they wished.[1] Practically the only occasion when the full Council assembles is on a demise of the Crown: then, after the Accession Council (a different and less precisely defined body) has declared the person entitled to succeed, the Privy Council meets to take the oath of allegiance and witness certain formalities required by law to be performed by the new Sovereign.

Ordinarily not more than three or four Councillors will be summoned, and all of these will usually be Ministers, unless it is

---

[1] There was a memorable exception in 1714, when Queen Anne lay dying. Two Whig dukes insisted on taking their places at the Council board, captured the vacant office of Lord Treasurer from the Tories, and set in train the process that secured the Hanoverian succession.

thought convenient to make up a quorum by bringing in the Queen's Private Secretary, who nowadays is always sworn of the Council so that there shall be no doubt of the propriety of giving him access to Cabinet secrets. They are shown into an ante-room of Buckingham Palace, and wait there until the Queen, who is in the adjoining room, rings her bell. Then the equerry on duty shows in the Lord President. In the Queen's room a table is set out, with chairs round it; but no one, at any stage in the proceedings, sits down.

The Lord President spends perhaps ten minutes answering the Queen's questions, showing her papers, and explaining exactly what business the Council is required to transact. Then the bell rings again, and the councillors file in one by one, the Clerk bringing up the rear. All shake hands with the Queen. She then takes her stand at the head of the table, and the councillors stand along the side of it to her right, the Lord President next to the Queen. The Clerk stands facing them. The Lord President reads through the list of appointments, consents, orders and other documents requiring the Queen's assent in Council, and to each item separately the Queen speaks the one word "Approved".

The Clerk, a permanent civil servant of the highest rank, who has prepared the whole, will then issue a printed announcement that, at a Council holden at Buckingham Palace on such and such a day, "present the Queen's Most Excellent Majesty in Council", and in accordance with the provisions of such and such statutes, these appointments were made or these orders given. They are then law. Councils of this pattern are held on the average about once a fortnight when Parliament is sitting.

It so happened that the hundredth Council of the reign was that which Mr. John Diefenbaker attended in December 1957, shortly after he had come to power as Prime Minister of Canada. He was sworn of the Council on that occasion, and witnessed the giving of the Queen's approval to certain amendments of the Canadian constitution—as is still necessary owing to the technicalities of the federal system, although it is well settled that nothing affecting Canada is to be done by the Queen through her United Kingdom machinery of state except at the request of Canada herself.

These periodic acts of participation by the Queen in the business of government as the supreme theoretical source of authority are conducted with the minimum of formality; her other main routine of collaboration with her statesmen is managed with no formality at all. As has been said in an earlier chapter, it is essential to the British scheme of life that the actual wielders of power must always be ready to explain and justify their doings with the utmost deference to the Queen, as representative of the common man and woman for whose benefit power is entrusted to them. Thus the head of every department of state should always be prepared at any time to come and speak for his department to the Queen; and occasionally for some special purpose he may be actually summoned to do so.

In practice, however, the result of her attempting to study each branch of administration separately would be to stereotype exactly that formalism which it is most desired to avoid. If a Minister allowed himself to become embarked on a general or far-ranging conversation with his Sovereign, he would continually find himself obliged to pull himself up and reply to some question: "I am sorry, Ma'am, but that lies within the responsibility of my colleague the Secretary for Such-and-Such Affairs. I have no commission to advise Your Majesty upon it, and it would not be proper for me to speak without first consulting him or asking Your Majesty to call for a report from his department". There would be an exchange of minutes between the departments and the cumbrous wheels of state would have to revolve before the Queen's curiosity could be satisfied.

Consequently it has long been the custom that the personal attendances of departmental Ministers at the Palace should be somewhat rare—that of the Chancellor of the Exchequer on the eve of his budget statement is one of the obviously exceptional cases—and that the Prime Minister should come at regular intervals and speak for all. It is very natural that he should do so; for his office, which was two centuries old before it was even recognized by the law to exist, grew out of the necessity for a regular chairman of Cabinet meetings when King George I ceased to attend them in person. He is almost as uninhibited in the range of subjects he may discuss as is the Queen herself—not quite, for he must occasionally be compelled to say "as to that, Ma'am, only your Canadian, or only your West Indian Ministers can advise you"—and therefore his conversations with her on United Kingdom politics can travel over the entire ground with complete ease and naturalness.

This system, which gives to the Prime Minister, on political subjects, a near monopoly of the royal ear, is not without its critics. There are some who think that there is already too great a tendency for the office of the Prime Minister to aggrandize itself at the expense of the rest of the Cabinet, and that other Ministers ought to have fuller opportunities of making themselves known to the Queen as political personalities in their own right.

Some day, after all, she may have to choose a new Prime Minister from among them; and although she does her best to pursue her acquaintance with them by inviting them to her table and by other strictly social means, that is not altogether a satisfactory substitute for the exploration of their thoughts on the subjects with which they are professionally concerned. Since this is not a treatise on constitutional law and custom, it is sufficient here to mention that the difference of opinion exists, without attempting to take sides in the dispute.

The present custom is for the Prime Minister to see the Queen about once a week when Parliament is sitting, usually on Tuesday, which is the day before the regular Cabinet meeting. During the fifth year of the Queen's reign, for example, he had thirty-four of these interviews. Since Sir Winston Churchill changed his wartime habit of lunching weekly with King George VI, the Prime Minister has generally arrived at the Palace at half-past six. He spends ten minutes with Sir Michael Adeane, the Principal Private Secretary, informing himself of any matters that may have arisen in his office during the week and on which the Prime Minister ought to have an opinion to offer to his Sovereign; then he is shown into the Queen's presence.

She always sees him, of course, quite alone, and what passes between them is entirely confidential. The Prime Minister never spends less than half an hour with Her Majesty, and usually he is in the Palace from half past six until eight o'clock. The Queen has of course read all the Cabinet minutes of the week, and it is reasonable to suppose that matters arising out of these supply the staple of her conversation with the head of her Government.

After the Prime Minister and the Lord President, the member of the Government of whom the Queen sees most is the Secretary of State for Foreign Affairs. This is partly because of the tradition that the Sovereign, as the representative of the nation to the outside world, takes a specially personal part in assisting its foreign relations: there is, for example, some truth in the popular legend that King Edward VII did much to smooth the path of his Ministers in negotiating the Entente Cordiale with the French Republic.

Whether the Queen has or has not many opportunities thus to sweeten intercourse with friendly Powers, she certainly feels herself specially bound to follow the Foreign Office telegrams carefully, if only to be able to converse intelligently with the numerous foreign ambassadors who come formally to present their credentials. On those occasions, it will be remembered, the Foreign Secretary is always present. He is also invariably in attendance when state visits are exchanged with the monarchs or presidents of foreign Powers. The conventions of international courtesy prescribe that a new Sovereign shall make and receive in the course of her reign one such formal visit to and from each foreign Power with which she is in friendly relations. The custom is not in fact extended to all, especially the more distant, countries; but it is so far regarded as binding that the Queen does not allow herself to travel informally in any country abroad before the formal visits have taken place.

This, for example, is the reason why she could not accompany the Duke of Edinburgh when he went to see the Brussels Exhibition of 1958: Queen Elizabeth and King Baldwin have not yet established themselves on "visiting terms". The custom, which is exactly analogous to that now dying out in England, of "leaving cards" on newcomers to a neighbourhood, may seem an anachronistic survival of a more ceremonious world; but while it persists it serves an amiable purpose by concentrating the resources of publicity upon the more attractive and friendly aspects of one foreign country after another. The special supplements in the newspapers, the fireworks and gala performances, the getting together of commercial people who follow in the train of royalty, all have their part to play in promoting international understanding.

Each of these visits, naturally, has its unique features, but they all follow the same general pattern, and the nature of the Queen's part in the proceedings will be sufficiently indicated by a single example. Let us take the state visit of the President of Portugal and Madame Craveiro Lopes in October 1955.

The President arrived in a Portuguese warship, the *Bartolomeu Dias*, and on approaching British waters was met by three of the Queen's frigates, which escorted him up the Channel. At the Nore, which the *Bartolomeu Dias* passed at a quarter past six in the morning of October 25, the Admiral commanding the station came on board to pay his respects, and a salute was fired by the guns of the battery at Sheerness. The whole squadron then steamed up the river to berth above Tower Bridge. Much the same stately compliments were paid to the Queen later on, when she, in a British ship, sailed up the Tagus to Lisbon.

Protocol requires that, at the moment when the distinguished visitor leaves his own ship to continue his journey in transport provided by the Queen, a member of the Royal Family shall receive him. Accordingly the Duke of Gloucester, accompanied by the Portuguese Ambassador, met the President on board the *Bartolomeu Dias* and transhipped with him into the British Royal Barge. This vessel, followed by others containing the President's suite and members of the Queen's Household attached to attend him during the visit, conveyed him to the pier at Westminster, under the shadow of the Houses of Parliament. Here the Queen herself was waiting to greet him, according to the rule of courtesy that his hostess should be the first person he meets on setting foot in her capital city, whether at a railway station or on a landing stage. With the Queen were all the members of the Royal Family in London—the Duke of Edinburgh, Queen Elizabeth the Queen Mother, Princess Margaret and the Duchesses of Gloucester and Kent.

After these had greeted the President a number of great dignitaries were presented to him, including the Prime Minister and several senior members of the Cabinet, the Lord Mayor of London, the General Officer Commanding the London District, and the Mayor of Westminster, in whose city the meeting was taking place. The President inspected a guard of honour of the Coldstream Guards and then a procession was formed to take him, with a Sovereign's Escort of the Household Cavalry, to Buckingham Palace, the Queen driving in the first carriage with the President and the Duke of Gloucester, and the Duke of Edinburgh in the second with Madame Lopes. At the Palace the visitors were conducted through ranks of the Gentlemen at Arms and the Yeomen of the Guard, and presented their suite to the Queen before being conducted to their rooms.

They were to stay three days, filled with a round of festivities and ceremonies. The Queen was not personally involved in all of these; but it is worth while to pass them in cursory review, because in foreign countries, where she is the guest instead of the hostess, a closely corresponding programme is always arranged for her.

On the first afternoon of the visit, then, the President and his lady laid a wreath on the grave of the Unknown Warrior in Westminster Abbey, visited the Queen Mother for half an hour at Clarence House, received formal addresses of welcome from the London County Council and the City of Westminster at St. James's Palace, and then visited their own Embassy in Belgrave Square. They were back at Buckingham Palace in time to be the guests of honour at a state banquet, at the end of which the Queen made a speech proposing the President's health and the President replied—both speeches, naturally, being devoted mainly to the theme of Anglo-Portuguese friendship and celebrating the ancient alliance which, with only one serious break, has continued since the fourteenth century.

On the second day the President received the High Commissioners of the Commonwealth and the heads of the Diplomatic Corps at Buckingham Palace before driving, with the Queen's own Sovereign's Escort and Standard, to be ceremonially entertained by the Lord Mayor and Corporation of London in Guildhall. In the afternoon they visited the winter exhibition of the Royal Academy and in the evening they gave a return dinner to the Queen and the Duke of Edinburgh at the Portuguese Embassy. The third day was in the main informal and they were able to visit various places of interest chosen by themselves, just as the Queen is also as a rule allowed one day of fairly normal sightseeing when she is a state guest in a foreign country. The Harwell atomic station figured in the President's programme; the Wallace Collection and a day nursery in Westminster in his wife's; and both attended a reception of the

Anglo-Portuguese Society. They dined quietly with the Queen and the Duke of Edinburgh at the Palace, and went on to hear a special performance of opera from the royal box at Covent Garden.

Finally, on the morning of Friday, October 28, they took leave of the Queen inside Buckingham Palace, and at that moment the state visit was over. On some occasions the leave-taking is only technical, and for this special purpose of putting an end to the ceremonial side. For example, at Oslo, the Queen and the Duke of Edinburgh carried through this formality in the royal palace and then, before sailing for home, entertained the King and Queen of Norway to a purely friendly family party on board the Royal Yacht lying in the harbour. But in the Portuguese case the timetable would not allow of this relaxation: the President and Madame Lopes had to drive straight to London Airport, in ordinary motor cars with all the pomp of the three preceding days laid away, and take flight home to Lisbon.

This then is the routine of a state visit, such as the heads of monarchies and republics alike are accustomed to pay to one another in the high courtesy of international relations. Queen Elizabeth II has already been guest and hostess in many of them.

As these pages are passing through the press she is entertaining Dr. Heuss, the President of the West German Federation—a remarkable token of reconciliation, and of the acceptance of the new Germany into the comity of the peace-loving western nations. Before very long, no doubt, she will be invited to pay a return visit to Bonn. She has already been the guest of nearly all the reigning Sovereigns of Northern Europe—of the Kings of Sweden, Denmark and Norway, and of Queen Juliana of the Netherlands. Nowhere has she been more grandly entertained than in Paris, where she stayed with President Coty in the Elysée Palace in the spring of 1957, and the beautiful city, perhaps for the first time since the tragic days of hostile occupation, decked itself in its gayest apparel, recapturing all its traditional glory of music and light to do the Queen of England honour. And in 1958 the Queen was in Washington, to renew the old friendship of her father with President Eisenhower, and to take part in the 350th anniversary celebration of the founding of the oldest State, Virginia, in an heroic adventure which is the most intimate and romantic of the ancestral memories that England and America share.

These formal appearances of the Queen as representative head of Kingdom and Commonwealth, in close association with the heads of other nations, are a spectacular means of concentrating the thoughts of her people for a little while upon the happier and friendlier side of international relations in a world distracted by hatred. There are other regular occasions when, with still more finely distilled pageantry, she displays herself before her subjects as the impersonation of their own historic prowess and fame. The best-known of these is the annual celebration of the day in June which is appointed to be kept, by a polite fiction, as her birthday—though actually she was born on April 21, 1926.

The ceremony of trooping the colour on Horse Guards Parade, Whitehall, derives from the military ritual by which, on the eve of action, the flag was carried successively along every rank of a seventeenth-century regiment, in order that each man might recognize the emblem to which he would rally in battle. As developed to its dramatic perfection by the Brigade of Guards, it is by general consent the noblest exhibition of disciplined movement to be seen anywhere in the modern world. Accompanied by the pomp of martial music, with the Queen to preside over the whole manoeuvre, receive the salute, and then ride home at the head of her troops along the processional way of the Mall, it holds up to the people an image of their whole tradition of valour and loyalty from Crecy to El Alamein.

Even more steeped in tradition and irradiated with the colours of history, though seen by a smaller company of people, is the annual festivity of the Knights of the Garter in Windsor

Castle. This also is a midsummer festival. At mid-day the Queen feasts with her Knights in St. George's Hall, having previously with her own hands invested the new Knights, if any there be, with the robes and insignia of the order in a private ceremony of great dignity.

After luncheon, robed like them in the great velvet mantle and plumed hat of the Order, she accompanies them in procession, attended by the Heralds, the Gentlemen at Arms, the Yeomen of the Guard, and the Military Knights who are the Third Estate of the Order of the Garter, through the wards of the ancient fortress-palace, to give thanks for all the glory of England in the superb chapel of her patron saint.

A ceremony of similar import is performed, though at less regular intervals, by the Queen and the Knights of the Thistle in their small chapel in St. Giles's Cathedral, Edinburgh. The symbolism is parallel in both cases: its public significance is the demonstration that the inmost recognition of great eminence in the service of the state, whether military or civil, consists in enrolment in the small circle of the great who are to be regarded as in a peculiar sense the personal companions of the Queen, as the first knights in 1348 were the companions of King Edward in battle. And if they are companions of the Queen they must be in fraternal relation to one another.

The Garter especially, the oldest secular order of Christian chivalry, in its present composition brings together the principal leaders of all three services in the second world war, with a few representatives of the ancient nobility of England, and three former Prime Ministers of different parties, Sir Winston Churchill, Lord Attlee and Sir Anthony Eden. The participation of this little band—the number of non-royal Knights is limited to twenty-five—in the great act of corporate dedication in June, is a public affirmation that among the leaders of the English all personal differences and rivalries are to be laid aside and forgotten in the presence of the Queen, who stands for the cause of the whole realm, in which all parties merge their separate aims.

The Order of the Garter, founded by King Edward III in order to revive the legendary glories of King Arthur's Round Table, passed through many vicissitudes, and at times became the sport of party politics and even of corruption before King George VI announced that he would henceforth nominate to its membership at his own discretion, without the constitutional advice of any Minister. He did the same with the Thistle, and with the modern Order of Merit, which had been founded by his grandfather, Edward VII. The Royal Victorian Order, being intended to reward personal service to the Sovereign, has always been conferred on this basis.

This does not mean, of course, that the Queen in choosing a person to be a Knight of the Garter or a companion of the Order of Merit is prevented from taking any one else into her confidence, or acts on impulse or caprice. She is constitutionally free to consult anyone she likes, and probably does discuss the question with more people than have an opportunity to express themselves about ordinary honours; but she need tell no one what she has done, and no one is responsible to Parliament for her selection. With other honours than these, however, the recommendations are filtered through the machinery of the various departments of state, and the whole list is finally edited in the office of the Prime Minister, and comes to her with his authority. She accepts it on his "advice", in the technical constitutional sense.

Nevertheless, the Queen is the sole fountain of honour, and though the effective decision to make an award may be taken by a Minister, its value for the recipient depends largely on the fact that it is actually and physically bestowed upon him by the hand of the Queen. She herself (unlike her predecessor Elizabeth I, who delegated this function to a male courtier) touches his shoulders with the sword of accolade, or pins the medal on his breast.

Long lists of honours are published twice a year, on New Year's Day and the Queen's fictitious Birthday; and after each there is a succession of investitures, varying in number but never less than five. It is a measure of the growing appetite for honours (or would it be kinder to suppose that it was the multiplication of merit in the people?) that even twenty years ago two investitures for each list sufficed. The investiture is generally held in the State Apartments of Buckingham Palace, and by an extremely popular innovation of King George VI, two guests are allowed to accompany each recipient of honour and watch the proceedings.

The Queen on these occasions is attended by the Yeomen of the Guard, and by her two Gurkha Orderly Officers. On her entry the National Anthem is played, after which the whole company sits down, and the Lord Chamberlain or other senior officer of the Household reads out the names one by one. If the award is of the Victoria Cross or the George Cross, he reads the full citation describing the act of bravery by which it has been earned.

The bearer of each name called files past the Queen, kneeling for the accolade if the honour of knighthood is to be conferred, otherwise standing while she takes the decoration from an equerry and pins it to his coat, or hangs it on a small hook previously sewn on his uniform for the purpose. To each she finds time to say some few words of personal appreciation. The whole ceremony takes about an hour and a quarter.

These, then, are the principal occasions on which the Queen stands out in majesty, as the visible Head of the State, symbolical of its history and its power. It remains to consider the rare circumstances in which she may have to act upon the state, not as a symbol, but with personal and determinant authority.

Once the machinery of government has provided her with a Prime Minister and Cabinet, enjoying the confidence of Parliament, her position as a constitutional monarch requires her to act always in accordance with the advice of her Ministers, and particularly of the Prime Minister, who has recommended them for appointment and ordinarily communicates their collective opinion to her. She may discuss their proposals in advance with them; she may do all in her power to persuade them, using the weight of special knowledge that she gradually accumulates by being always in the inner counsels of the state while Ministries come and go; she may be informally an important adviser in private of those who are formally her advisers. But when their advice takes formal shape, she has no choice but to accept it.

Circumstances, however, can arise in which the Queen is without a Government, or her Government has lost the support of Parliament. The simplest case is when the Prime Minister dies in office (as has not happened since the death of Lord Palmerston in 1865) or resigns for ill-health or other non-political reasons while still undefeated in the House of Commons.

By constitutional convention, when a Prime Minister resigns, the whole of his Cabinet and the Ministers outside the Cabinet resign with him. There is therefore for the moment nobody whose advice the Queen is constitutionally bound to take. She has to provide herself with a new Government, and that quickly, if the machinery of administration is not to come to a standstill—although it is customary for the outgoing Ministers to remain in their departments and keep the routine going, while scrupulously postponing any decision that might be thought controversial. In finding a Government, the Queen first selects a Prime Minister and then asks him to submit to her the names of the colleagues he wishes to be appointed to the various Cabinet and other offices. It is only the first step, therefore, that is personal to her; but in that step, the choice of a Prime Minister, she is untrammelled. She may consult whom she likes; she need not consult anybody at all.

The Queen has already been in this position twice. The first occasion was when Sir Winston Churchill resigned, on no other grounds than the advance of old age. As a veteran servant of the Royal House, he had thought it his duty to remain in office long enough to see his master's daughter crowned and fully established in the seat of King George VI, as Lord Melbourne did with Queen Victoria, and to withdraw when a younger man was clearly designated for the succession and could move into his place without jolt or jar. That position he judged to have been reached in April, 1955, and he then made way, with the moral certainty that Sir Anthony Eden would succeed him, as not only he but the Conservative Party as a whole had long taken for granted. That would be his advice if the Queen should ask him to recommend a new Prime Minister.

It is nevertheless important to note that the Queen was under no obligation to ask for his advice, or to follow it if given; for his commission to advise with constitutional authority expired at the moment when his resignation was accepted. It is well known that when Mr. Gladstone ended his long career Queen Victoria did not consult him about the succession and in fact appointed in Lord Rosebery a Minister who would certainly not have been Mr. Gladstone's choice.

When the outgoing Prime Minister happened to be a statesman enjoying the supreme moral authority and international fame of Sir Winston Churchill, no one of course doubts that the Queen must have consulted him, and probably nobody else. But she need not have done so and it was not explicitly stated that she had; for by a wholesome convention no public disclosure is made of precisely what happens in these intensely confidential negotiations, and their purport is only allowed to transpire, for the benefit of historians, after a discreet number of years has elapsed.

A markedly different situation occurred when Sir Anthony in turn had to resign less than two years later. Although he had been visibly wilting under the strain of office, the eventual physical collapse came quite suddenly: he had to be carried off for immediate surgical care and was in no condition to give the Queen any help in forming a new Government even if she had asked for it. Moreover, two of his subordinates, Mr. R. A. Butler and Mr. Harold Macmillan, had very closely balanced claims to be considered the successor most likely to command the allegiance of the party in office. No one but the Queen could choose between them.

The Queen gave to her choice very careful attention, and certainly did not act without reference to the most weighty opinion available. During the day when she was finally making up her mind she summoned to her side the two among the senior leaders of the Conservative Party who were not themselves eligible to be Prime Minister—Sir Winston Churchill, because he had already retired on the ground of old age, and Lord Salisbury, because he was incapable of sitting in the House of Commons and there is now general agreement, scarcely amounting to a binding constitutional convention, that a twentieth-century Government cannot be led from the House of Lords. Many writers have taken it for granted that these two elder statesmen in fact dictated the Queen's choice. There is no evidence to justify this assumption. Although no one else of comparable eminence saw the Queen that day, she did not approach her task with a blank mind. For several weeks past the probability of Sir Anthony Eden's withdrawal had been apparent and it would have been impossible for the Queen not to be thinking about what she would do when the time came. It is reasonable to suppose that she had discussed the problem with Sir Anthony himself at some of his weekly audiences. No Minister is entitled to give advice that will bind the Sovereign at some future date when he himself will no longer be in office; but Sir Anthony's views, informally and confidentially expressed, would inevitably be remembered by the Queen and would carry with her the weight of his profound knowledge of the parliamentary background.

One of the main factors to be taken into account in choosing between two rival candidates would be the state of feeling inside their party: a durable Government would not easily be formed if the rank and file were resentful of the choice of the wrong man to lead them. It is therefore important for the Sovereign to know something of the minds of the people—such as the Whips—whose special business it is to be in close touch with party feeling. It would not be seemly for her to send for the Chief Whip and discuss such matters directly with him, especially at a time when she still had a Prime Minister in office. But her private secretaries can see anyone they like, high or humble, without publicity; and it may be presumed that during those weeks before the resignation a considerable number of men and women who might be able to illuminate one or another facet of the problem unburdened themselves in the discreet room in the North wing of Buckingham Palace where Sir Michael Adeane collects all possible opinions that may help the Queen to make a decision. When Sir Winston Churchill and Lord Salisbury called at the Palace on the day, it is quite possible that she had already decided in favour of Mr. Macmillan, and wished only to make these two old servants of her father the first to share her confidence, to ask for their approval of her choice and their support for her new Prime Minister. All that is certain is that Lord Salisbury did assent to her decision, for he immediately took office under Mr. Macmillan; what share, if any, he and Sir Winston had had in determining it will not be known for some time.

The issue between Mr. Macmillan and Mr. Butler was not a mere matter of personal rivalry. The two statesmen were representative of different shades of thought within the Conservative Party, and the Queen's choice between them, in an evenly balanced situation, was bound to deflect the policy of the new Government in one direction or another. The ever-present possibility of having to make such a momentous decision at short notice is one of the reasons why it is essential for the Queen to maintain her laborious study of departmental and parliamentary documents and keep herself continuously responsive to every change in the political weather.

In choosing a Prime Minister the Queen does not act as a mere agent, interpreting the mind of the party that happens to be in power. She is the representative of the whole realm, indeed of the Commonwealth, and may properly take larger factors into consideration. For example in 1923, when King George V selected Mr. Baldwin in preference to Lord Curzon, whom the Conservative Party had almost unanimously expected to succeed, he was probably influenced by the thought that Baldwin was likely to preserve a milder temper in relations between the parties than Curzon, who was detested by most of the Labour Opposition. (The reason given at the time, that it was impossible to have a Prime Minister in the Lords, is thought to have been suggested by Lord Stamfordham to spare Curzon humiliation, although it now tends to be cited as a constitutional precedent.)

This is part of the answer to the Socialist critics who objected to the procedure adopted on the resignation of Sir Anthony Eden, on the ground that it embarrassed the Queen by dragging her into party politics. The Conservatives, they maintained, should have elected a new leader, who they implied would automatically become Prime Minister. But the whole constitutional history of England is against them. Even if the Conservatives had so acted, their elected candidate would have had no automatic right of succession. No party is entitled to deprive the Queen of her freedom of choice. It is true that when a party comes fresh from victory in a general election, the Queen could in practice do no other than send for the leader under whom it has won the fight. But in those circumstances the leader comes with the authority of the people, not merely of the party caucus.

It is true also that at all times the general wish of the party is the weightiest single factor to be taken into consideration; the

Queen cannot have a Prime Minister whom his party in the House of Commons will not follow. But when there is more than one possible leader who, with the additional prestige that the royal nomination can give him, would be able to command sufficient support to give him a majority in the House of Commons, then the constitution leaves it to the Sovereign's personal judgment to decide between them, and to do so if she wishes on grounds that have nothing to do with party at all. (She could, for example, with perfect propriety, ask one of the Dominion High Commissioners "which of these two, whose claims seem to me almost exactly equal, would be the more likely to sweeten relations between my Governments here and in your country?")

If her judgment is in error, the party can always have the last word. The chosen Prime Minister may come back in a day or two and say that, having consulted the other principal personalities of his party, he finds that so few of them will consent to take office under his leadership that he cannot form a Government; he therefore resigns his commission and the Queen must try again with someone else. But the party has no right to the *first* word. A party might force the Sovereign's hand by entering into a compact in advance that none of its members, if invited to do so, should consent to form a Government until the party had elected a leader and that none should take office under any other Prime Minister than he. This would be effective; but it would be none the less unconstitutional and disrespectful to the Queen.

Not all Prime Ministers resign while they are still, but for personal circumstances such as ill health or old age, masters of the political arena. It may happen that the Government has been defeated in the House of Commons on some important motion which it has treated as "a question of confidence". Under the rigid conditions of party discipline that have been developed in the twentieth century, this happens much less frequently than in Queen Victoria's times; but it remains a possibility. The convention is that after such an adverse vote the defeated Government can no longer work with that House of Commons: there must be either a new Government or a new House, or both.

It is for the Prime Minister to decide whether he will resign or advise the Queen to dissolve Parliament and order a general election. But inasmuch as he no longer speaks for the House of Commons, but only for himself and his colleagues, his advice has less constitutional weight than before confidence was withdrawn; and the Queen can in certain circumstances decline it without impropriety. That is to say, she may side provisionally with her Parliament against her Prime Minister. If, being defeated, he asks for a dissolution, she may reply that before granting his request she must have an opportunity to discover whether any other statesman is capable of forming a Government to which the House of Commons will give its confidence.

This in effect would force the Prime Minister to resign and the Queen would then send for the leader of the Opposition and ask him to take office. If he in his turn had to report inability to form a Government, the Queen would have to recall her original Ministers and accept their advice to dissolve. She would have somewhat compromised her royal dignity, so that the power of refusing a dissolution to a defeated Minister is one to be used with very great caution—practically, only when the Sovereign is quite sure that an alternative Government will be able to carry on.

Lord Byng, wielding as Governor-General of Canada in 1926 the same powers as belong to the Sovereign in the United Kingdom, refused a dissolution to the defeated Government, brought the Opposition into office, and then had to dissolve on the advice of his new Ministers. He set on foot a controversy that has scarcely yet been closed, and his motives were impugned in a way that would do disastrous damage to the monarchy, which has to be superior to all party considerations, if the Queen herself were similarly criticized.

Nevertheless circumstances proper for the use of the power may still arise on occasion. An example might easily have occurred in 1924. At the end of the previous year Mr. Baldwin's Conservative Government had lost heavily at the polls, and came back to Westminster without a majority, though still the largest of the three parties in the House of Commons. Mr. Baldwin decided not to resign until actually defeated in a parliamentary vote, in order to make the smallest party, Mr. Asquith's Liberals, declare their attitude and take the responsibility of bringing Labour to power for the first time. On the first division the Liberals duly combined with the Labour party to defeat the Government; Mr. Baldwin resigned, and Mr. Ramsay MacDonald took office. But at the end of the year, on another issue of confidence, Asquith took the side of Baldwin and the Labour Ministry in its turn was defeated. Thereupon MacDonald advised the King to dissolve Parliament.

Now if the circumstances had been only slightly different— that is to say, if Baldwin had chosen to resign immediately after the preceding general election, before Parliament met—King George V might very well have thought it proper to reject MacDonald's advice. He might have said that the new Parliament was not yet a year old, and it was preposterous to part with it until he had tested the new alliance of the Liberals with the Conservatives, to see whether it would persist and be firm enough to support another Baldwin administration. But as it was, that early vote against the Conservatives stood on the record. This House of Commons had not only censured the Labour Party; it had previously censured the Conservatives too; and the Liberals were clearly too few to be able to produce a Government. Therefore nothing more could be done with it, and the King acceded to MacDonald's advice and granted a dissolution.

Seven years later, when MacDonald again ran into a parliamentary storm, King George did demur to his Prime Minister's first proposal. The Labour Cabinet had been fatally split by the great financial crisis of 1931 and MacDonald wished to resign and advise the King to send for the Conservative leader—still Mr. Baldwin. But the King persuaded him to withdraw his resignation and form a new Government combining the few Labour men who remained faithful to their leader with the Conservative and Liberal chiefs in a national coalition to attempt to save the gold standard (in which they failed) and surmount the crisis.

Every change of Government has its own unique features; but these examples of the way in which the personal intervention of the Sovereign has helped to mould events in the comparatively recent past will serve to suggest how the Queen might be called upon to act on comparable future occasions.

A few words should be added about the Queen's part in the formal process of a change of Government. In its simplest form the Prime Minister in office has been defeated at the polls in a general election and, though under no obligation to give way until the House of Commons has met and confirmed the judgment of the constituencies, decided to resign at once—as Mr. Attlee did in 1951. He requests an audience of the Queen, which is immediately granted, comes to Buckingham Palace and begs leave to resign his charge. The Queen accepts his resignation, and in thanking him for his past services will in all probability offer to raise him to the dignity of an earl. Mr. Attlee preferred to remain in the House of Commons, but accepted the honour a few years later.

The next step, if the Queen is in no difficulty about deciding on the succession, is to send her private secretary to summon the leader of the Opposition to her presence. He comes and she asks him if he is prepared to form a government. He accepts the commission and "kisses hands on appointment as Prime Minister and First Lord of the Treasury". He then goes away to consult his friends and distribute offices in the new Cabinet.

Let it be assumed that he succeeds in assembling a suitable

team to carry on the administration. He submits the list of names to the Queen—coming himself to explain it to her—and having obtained her formal consent allows it to be published. Then, and not till then, the outgoing Ministers of the old Government are sent for to Buckingham Palace or Windsor Castle, where they take leave of the Queen and give back into her hands their seals or other insignia of office.

Very shortly afterwards, sometimes later on the same day, the incoming Ministers are received. If any of those entering the Cabinet are not already Privy Councillors, a Council is held at which they take the oath. The Queen hands her new Ministers their seals, insignia, or instruments of appointment, and they disperse to take over their departments. The final act is usually the submission of a short list of "resignation honours" for members and supporters of the fallen Government, which is drawn up by the outgoing Prime Minister, but granted by the Queen on the constitutional advice of his successor, who in the comity of British politics is always ready to do this courtesy to his defeated adversary.

One other personal function of the Queen in government, which few people expect will ever need to be exercised again, cannot be wholly ignored. Even when her Government and her Parliament are in agreement with one another, she is still entitled, acting on no-one's advice, to dismiss the Government or to dissolve Parliament. The two come to the same thing: for if she dismisses the Government she must also get rid of a House of Commons which would certainly overthrow any alternative Ministry she might instal; and if she dissolves a Parliament that supports the Government, the Cabinet will have been so slighted that they can do no other than resign.

The power has not been exercised since 1834, when William IV dismissed his Whig Ministers, called upon Sir Robert Peel to replace them and on his advice dissolved Parliament. After being confirmed in office by victory in the general election, Peel

165

laid down in Parliament the constitutional doctrine, still held to be valid, that by accepting the commission in these circumstances he had made himself retrospectively responsible to Parliament for everything that the King had done during the interval, including the decisive step of dismissing the Whigs. But if Peel had lost the election the position of King William, and even of the monarchy itself, would have been left extremely precarious.

Could this power nevertheless be asserted in modern conditions? Only, it would seem, in dire emergency, and as a last defence of the constitution. But let us suppose that, in some violent outburst of emotion such as may sweep even the most level-headed nation, an unscrupulous demagogue of the Hitler type manages to get himself returned at a general election with a majority in the House of Commons. He then sets about to establish a totalitarian regime. Pressing to their full extent his powers of advising the Queen, he insists on her creating enough peers of his following to give him command of the House of Lords. Next he drives through both Houses legislation depriving all his opponents of their seats, and declaring that in future elections only one party, his own, shall be permitted to nominate candidates. Finally, he produces a Bill repealing the limitation of five years on the duration of Parliament, making the existing House indissoluble, and giving it (or himself) the power to fill up its own vacancies without by-elections.

All this sounds fantastic; but it is substantially the process by which Fascist and Communist revolutions are accomplished and, as far as legal forms go, there is nothing in the British constitution to stop it once the first step, the winning of the general election, is granted. Nothing, that is, except one thing—the royal prerogative. At some stage in the progress of the revolutionary torrent the Queen could call a halt.

She would have to judge her moment shrewdly, when she felt sure that the country had recovered from its temporary aberration and was ready to stop the rot. She would then dismiss the would-be dictator and call upon a more responsible statesman to form a Government. On the advice of this new Prime Minister she would dissolve Parliament and the ensuing general election would be fought openly on the issue, "the Queen against totalitarianism".

If she had judged the feeling of the people aright, her chosen Government would win the election and she would have saved the liberties of the country. But if she were mistaken, and her Government were defeated, her own position would be irretrievable. She would have descended into the party arena and been revealed as out of accord with the majority of her people; there would be no resource left but abdication.

Thus this prerogative power to dismiss a Government or dissolve Parliament on the Queen's own initiative is one only to be invoked in an emergency so extreme that it is justifiable and necessary to stake the very existence of the monarchy on a bid to thwart revolution. But in the circumstances imagined the survival of the monarchy as the puppet of a totalitarian regime would be blasphemy against its very nature, for it is the ultimate trustee of liberty. The possibility of this last desperate throw for freedom needs always to be kept in reserve, little as any believer in the sanity of England may think that it can ever have to be used. For if Britain should ever renounce its faith in liberty, it would be best and most honourable for the ancient monarchy to perish in the holocaust of freedom.

The Cost of Royalty

The Cost of Royalty

Monarchy is not the cheapest form of government: both the public pageantry and the extensive hospitality which are part of its service to the life of the people are bound to cost more than the comparatively drab regimes of republican states. But the question how much more it costs to have a Queen than it would cost to maintain the elected official who might be imagined in her place is not susceptible of a precise answer.

The oversea nations of the Commonwealth, whose bonds of union with one another depend so much on the Queen's person, have the monarchy for practically nothing. They pay the local expenses of royal tours, but that is all. With this exception, the cost of the monarchy is borne by the United Kingdom. This is no doubt fair, so long as the United Kingdom enjoys its present preferential treatment as the normal residence of the Sovereign. But a case might be made out for distributing such expenses as those of the Royal Yacht, the main purpose of which is to facilitate the journeys of the Queen, and other members of the Royal Family from time to time deputizing for her, about the Commonwealth. It is perhaps unfortunate that this vessel is called a yacht, which suggests a luxurious pleasure-ship, and has consequently been criticized as an extravagance. It is in fact seldom used for pleasure. Even when it carries the Royal Family northward for their summer holiday at Balmoral, use is made of it to enable them to visit the Queen's subjects on the western shores. Thus in August 1958 the newly created Prince of Wales was able to pay his first visit as such to his principality. Otherwise it is used practically solely for important official voyages in the national and imperial service. It belongs to and is manned by the Royal Navy, and ship and men (the former as a hospital ship) would be mobilized for active service, like the ceremonial troops who mount guard at Buckingham Palace and Windsor, in case of war. The Royal Navy of Great Britain has always borne the principal responsibility for the defence of the seaways of the Commonwealth, and the provision of the Royal Yacht is thrown in.

There is a sense in which it might be argued that the monarchy costs the country nothing at all: it can support itself out of its private resources. This is the result of its long continuous history. The constitutional theory of feudal England (as of all the contemporary monarchies of the Continent) was that the King was the universal landlord, managing the country as his estate through subordinate dignitaries who were rewarded with grants of land, and paying the expenses of government out of the rents of the "demesne"—that is, the property he retained in his own hand. Taxation began only as an exceptional device: when the King was faced with extraordinary expenditure, as in time of war, he turned to his faithful subjects for a grant to help him carry on.

With the passage of the centuries the extraordinary became the ordinary. The cost of government swelled continually, taxation had to provide for practically all, and the remnant of the Crown lands, much of which had been alienated, remained charged only with the upkeep of the monarchy itself. These lands still exist, and their present yield would pay the expenses of the monarchy twice over.

But even if this situation had not been modified in the way to be described below, it would not be quite honest to argue that the Queen is a rich woman by inheritance, who gives her public services for nothing. Since taxes are in constitutional theory free grants made by subjects to the Sovereign, the revenue from the Crown lands has always been tax-free: the King cannot pay taxes to himself. If the Queen's ancestors had been private persons, their incomes would have been progressively taxed, and in the last few reigns the death-duties would have been lethal. The great landed estate of her ancestors would have been wiped out before it reached the Queen. Her endowment to-day must be regarded as owed to the special exemptions of her ancestors *because* they were Kings and Queens. If she lived upon it, she would be supported by the accumulated taxes that the constitutional convention has caused the Treasury to forgo.

As a matter of fact she does not live upon it—or not directly. Since the time of William IV it has been customary for the Sovereign at the beginning of the reign to surrender the Crown lands, for his or her lifetime, to be managed by government Commissioners. The Treasury takes the revenue for the Consolidated Fund, and Parliament in return provides the Queen with an annual income, called the Civil List. She does not, however, part with the revenues of the Duchy of Lancaster, which since the fifteenth century has been a separate private estate of the Sovereign; and her eldest son as Duke of Cornwall is entitled to the revenues of that Duchy. Each of the two Duchies brings in an income of about £90,000 a year. But until the Prince of Wales is eighteen only one ninth of the revenue of the Duchy of Cornwall is retained for his maintenance, and from then until he comes of age his income is limited to £30,000. The remainder is handed over to the Treasury to be set against the Civil List.

The junior members of the Royal Family have fixed incomes assigned to them by Parliament, payable out of the Consolidated Fund and subject to income tax. Since they are all expected to share in their degree in the Queen's work as the national representative ("We're not a family, we're a firm", said King George VI) they are in effect salaried public servants. The Duke of Edinburgh receives a separate allowance of £40,000.

The Civil List voted by Parliament on the accession of Queen Elizabeth II was as follows:

	£
Her Majesty's Privy Purse	60,000
Salaries of Her Majesty's Household and retired allowances	185,000
Expenses of Her Majesty's Household . . .	121,000
Royal Bounty, alms and special services . .	13,200
Supplementary Provision	95,000

(The total is £474,200; the revenues collected by the Commissioners of Crown Lands certainly do not fall short of £1,000,000). The supplementary provision was inserted in order to provide against the necessity of a fresh application to Parliament in case of serious inflation, and also to give the Queen a fund of £25,000 from which she might provide for members of the Royal Family who did not have grants from the Consolidated Fund and yet were precluded by their position from taking up remunerative employment. Any part of it which is not needed in the year is returned to the Treasury.

Of the other items it is clear that the salaries and pensions, which in a monarchy are paid to members of the Household, would be equally required for the civil servants who in a republic would make up the personal staff of the head of the State. The other expenses of the Household are largely accounted for by the upkeep of the royal residences. How much money a republic would actually save by turning Windsor Castle into a museum and Buckingham Palace into a block of flats, and selling Balmoral and Sandringham, is a matter of speculation; but a President living in the counterparts of 10 Downing Street and Chequers would undoubtedly be cheaper. The Royal Bounty comes directly back to the people.

There remains the Privy Purse of £60,000. Mr. Humphry Berkeley, in a very able brief sketch of the royal finances, published in the *National and English Review* for August 1957, compares this with the salary of 100,000 dollars, with all expenses found, received by the President of the United States. The Queen's income is certainly more, justifiably more, as Mr. Berkeley argues. But even he has overlooked that the real cost of the Presidency is very much more than the annual salary. What sends up the bill is the cost of replacement. Every four years millions of dollars are poured out in a frenzy of deafening propaganda through conventions, primaries, and the presidential election itself before a new President can be installed.

It is true that these millions do not come out of the taxes; but through one channel or another Americans collectively have to pay them, and the ultimate charge on the national wealth comes to the same thing. The only corresponding expense of replacement in a hereditary system would seem to be an occasional obstetrician's fee; and that is no addition to the cost of monarchy, for it comes out of the Privy Purse. The worth of the monarchy to the Commonwealth is not for accountants to assess; but even in pounds, shillings and pence it is not self-evident that the change to republican institutions would in the long run be an economy.

The Queen
in the Commonwealth

The Queen in the Commonwealth

The Statute of Westminster, 1931, translating into legal shape the resolutions of the Imperial Conference of 1926, invested the principal Parliaments of the British Commonwealth of Nations—subject to their own voluntary adoption of the operative clauses—with sovereign control of all their national affairs. Henceforth neither the Ministers nor the Parliament at Westminster could issue any command to the countries named—which were Ireland, Canada, Newfoundland, Australia, New Zealand and South Africa; with the proviso that the application of some parts of the Act to some of these countries was postponed until they had themselves adopted it as they all eventually did. There were certain formal exceptions, in that the co-operation of the Imperial Parliament was still required to sanction the amendment of written federal constitutions; but since it was accepted from the beginning that this power was to be exercised only on the request and in accordance with the wish of the country concerned, the principle was not affected.

Each Parliament of the Commonwealth has unlimited legislative power in its country, and the Ministers responsible to it may pursue any foreign policy it will tolerate, without necessarily regarding the wishes of any other Government in the Commonwealth. But inasmuch as every Parliament then consisted of the Sovereign and two Houses (New Zealand has since abolished its second chamber), the legal unity of the Commonwealth was left solely residing in the person of the King, who was the one element common to all the legislative assemblies.

It is true that it was actually a Governor-General who convened the Houses and exercised all the royal functions in them; but this high officer was appointed as a personal representative of the King. The Statute contained a preamble declaring the constitutional doctrine that no change should be made in the rules of the royal succession except by the unanimous consent of all the sovereign members of the Commonwealth. Consequently it was possible to say that the unity of the Commonwealth now depended upon the allegiance of all its members to the same indivisible Crown.

There have been a number of changes in this system since 1931. Ireland and Burma have at their own request left the Commonwealth. Names of other nations have been added to those enumerated in the Statute of Westminster—India, Pakistan, Ceylon, Ghana, Malaya—while several more, such as the Central African Federation, the West Indian Federation and Nigeria, are expected to reach equal status with the rest in a short time. Of the four members in Asia, India and Pakistan have become republics, and Ceylon is in process of devising a republican constitution. These countries no longer regard the Crown as their link in the old sense with the Commonwealth: for them, the Queen is not the head of their own state, but of an association of states to which they belong. She has no function in their internal affairs, social or political. Malaya has a native monarchy of its own within the Commonwealth.

Moreover, the theory of an indivisible Crown has broken down. After the death of King George VI the members of the Commonwealth oversea all or nearly all desired, and all were accorded, the right to assign different local titles to the Queen. Although all these titles have something in common—at least the Queen's name and the expression "Head of the Commonwealth"—their variety compels us to think less of one indivisible Crown than of a series of Crowns all worn on one head. Consequently, more emphasis then ever is placed on the fact that the real bond of unity in the Commonwealth, or at least among its royalist members, is allegiance not to the Crown, which is a constitutional metaphor for the executive power in government, but to the Queen personally.

The Crown possesses exactly the same functions in each of these realms of the Commonwealth oversea as it has in the United Kingdom. It is the formal head of the legislature, the executive and the judiciary, the initiating force in all government. But the whole of these formal functions is exercised by the Governor-General; and although he is the Queen's personal representative, she has no personal part in choosing him. She simply appoints the candidate recommended by her Government on the spot, just as she accepts as her representative in the City of London the Lord Mayor elected by the citizens. Bills become Acts by the Royal Assent; but it is the Governor-General who gives it, without need to consult the Queen. And it is the Governor-General, not the Queen herself, who will if need be exercise the two remaining personal powers of the Sovereign in politics which were set out in the last chapter—the power to choose a new Prime Minister, and the power to give or withhold a dissolution of Parliament, which is tantamount to the right in emergency to dismiss a Government.

The upshot of all this is that the Queen does nothing personally in the *politics* of the nations over which she reigns beyond the United Kingdom. And since it has already been said that the bond of unity between them depends upon her personality, and not on the abstract institution we call the Crown, it follows that in these realms, even more than in the Mother Country, her supreme significance is social, not political.

A Governor-General can be a perfectly efficient head of the state; but as head of society he is inadequate for peoples who have grown up in the British Empire and breathe the atmosphere of monarchy as a way of life. Their sense of kinship with one another, and with their fellow-subjects of the same allegiance in other lands, requires an object of personal devotion, such as they cannot find in the temporary holder of political office, but only in affectionate loyalty to a person exalted above all partisan politics. And, although the royal person is in one sense a splendid symbol of the national and imperial life, the sentiment that gives the symbol meaning cannot be directed wholly to an abstraction. It clamours for relationship to a being of flesh and blood, who can be seen and known.

Wonderful indeed it is that the British nations oversea are able to sustain their loyalty so long by faith rather than by sight. But it is unjust to expect them to be satisfied with devotion to a Queen who is merely a portrait head on the coins and the postage stamps, a name to be prayed for in church and sung about in the National Anthem, a remote figure of ceremony whose doings they may read of in the newspapers. They need to see her face to face; the terms of the Statute of Westminster give them an equal right with the United Kingdom to do so, and the new mobility of the air age has made it far more possible than hitherto to gratify their desire.

It is not, however, by any means easy to give practical effect to the theoretical equality of all Commonwealth countries in relation to the person of the Queen. There are now six, in the course of the next few years there may well be nine, of these countries in which she is the head of the national life. If mathematical equality is to be literally applied, she should spend one-ninth of her time in each of them, arriving among them and settling down in their midst as the head and centre of society exactly as she now does in the United Kingdom. To give reality to such a conception she would need to stay for substantial periods—say, at least a year at a time. The apparatus of a court would grow up around her, not perhaps on the English scale, for the younger nations have simpler ways, but it would mean a substantial addition to the elaborations of public life. At least one official residence would have to be provided, and a use found for it during the eight years out of nine when the Queen was not in residence.

Meanwhile the United Kingdom would be left under a Governor-General, presumably moving between Buckingham Palace and Windsor and doing his best to fill the yawning social gap that the Queen's absence would leave.

All this, it must be acknowledged, would be perfectly fair, and the United Kingdom, having conceded equality to the sister nations, has no right to cling to its position of privilege in relation to the monarchy. Indeed, it is by no means improbable that some such geographical diffusion of the monarchy may be accomplished in generations to come. But if a serious attempt were made to establish it now, it is more than probable that the most vigorous objections would come not from the United Kingdom but from the oversea countries themselves. Theoretically, no doubt, the Commonwealth is to be regarded as an interlacing network, every national focus of which is linked by lines of equal calibre and tension with every other focus.

Actually, the lines are far more inclined to run radially to and from a single centre, and that centre is in London. All questions of status apart, there is still an instinctive reliance of all the younger communities of the Commonwealth upon the senior partner to maintain for them a permanent meeting-place and clearing-house of their mutual relations. In London Canadians and South Africans and Rhodesians, Australians and New Zealanders, still expect to find themselves on their visits in touch with the Commonwealth as a whole; there the relationship is multilateral, whereas in one another's capitals it is apt to be bilateral only. This conception of the old country as common ground for all its children may not derive directly from the presence of the Queen there; it depends on ancient habit and tradition. Nevertheless the Queen is the appointed embodiment of the tradition.

The Commonwealth no longer has a capital, in the sense of

a supreme seat of government, but it has for its peoples a geographical centre, which is in Buckingham Palace. It has also a spiritual centre in the person of the Queen; and, as has been said in previous chapters, she may carry that spiritual centre with her to any point of the geographical circumference that she visits. But the instinct of the Commonwealth insists that the spiritual centre shall never be long removed from the geographical, lest the shape of the whole become distorted.

Visitors from the Commonwealth to England expect to see the Queen. If she is making a tour oversea, they will no doubt postpone their visit against her return. But if, for example, a West Indian comes to London and is told that Her Majesty is at present living in Accra, and after another eight months there will be going on for a year to Canberra, it is unlikely that he will revise his plans in order to follow this peripatetic monarchy. And even if he did, he would incline to feel a stranger in the presence of the Queen of Ghana or Australia, in contrast to the sense he has in London of having come to pay his respects to a Sovereign who is as much his own as she is Queen of the dwellers in Berkeley Square. In a rapidly changing Commonwealth this diagnosis of the peoples' psychology may in a generation or so become obsolete; but few will dispute that it represents the general feeling to-day, and while this feeling persists it is inevitable that the Queen must continue to treat one country of the Commonwealth, the oldest, as her normal place of residence. In each of the others, or at least in each which remains a monarchy, she is at home; but inevitably her appearances in them must be occasional interludes in the general routine of her life.

These interludes, however, are of the very highest importance to the relationship of the Queen and her subjects, and so to the health of the body of the Empire. Every step that has been taken in the present century to relax the formal bonds between the United Kingdom and what were once dependencies has increased the urgency of frequent intercourse between the

Sovereign and the peoples oversea; and from the reign of King George V onwards this urgency has been progressively emphasized by the Sovereigns themselves, who have planned to make their travels in the Commonwealth ever more frequent and systematic. The present Queen, either before or since her accession, has made herself personally acquainted with all the self-governing kingdoms of which she is the head, except Ghana, where on the invitation of Dr. Nkrumah she is expected in 1959, and with many of the colonies that have yet to attain independent rank.

In the opening chapter it has been related how, in the year of her coming of age, she travelled with her father and mother through the length and breadth of the Union of South Africa, in the High Commission Territories of Basutoland, Swaziland and Bechuanaland, and in what were then the separate states of Southern and Northern Rhodesia. In the last months of her father's life she traversed Canada, with the Duke of Edinburgh, from ocean to ocean; and she was actually in Kenya when the news of his death summoned her to the Throne. She had flown to Kenya as the first stage in a great imperial mission, which was intended to take her round the world and through three of the kingdoms of the Commonwealth, as deputy for the King himself, who for years had been planning this grand progress but had been repeatedly prevented by ill-health from carrying out the plan.

Since her accession to the Throne the Queen has gone far to complete her knowledge of the wide dominion over which she reigns. In 1956 she was in Nigeria, a country still awaiting a true federal union of its three diverse sections before being admitted to the status of an independent member of the Commonwealth. Since its boundaries were fixed less by any pre-existing nationality than by the external convenience of the nineteenth-century Empire, its capacity to survive as an integrated community when the imperial scaffolding is removed may come to depend on the depth of feeling for the monarchy that can be engendered among its heterogeneous races; and this no doubt was a reason for choosing Nigeria, rather than any of the East African colonies, as the destination of the only journey the Queen has yet made for the sole benefit of a single state of the dependent Empire. She made history on that occasion by appointing two Nigerians as equerries—the first natives of Africa ever to be admitted to the intimate circle of the Royal Household.

In 1957 she paid her second visit to Canada, and her first as Queen; and here again she established a new precedent by being the first Sovereign to take her seat in person on her Canadian Throne and open in state a session of the Federal Parliament at Ottawa. But by far the most important of her imperial progresses hitherto was that of 1953–54, in which the long-cherished design of King George VI, after his repeated disappointments, was brought at last to accomplishment. It was the first time in history that the reigning Sovereign of any nation had travelled right round the world.

In a journey of 50,000 miles, the Queen with the Duke of Edinburgh, starting by air, made a short stop in Jamaica, where representatives of the other West Indian islands had assembled to greet them; sailed in the liner *Gothic* through the Panama Canal and across the Pacific Ocean; were entertained to the exotic feasting and revelry of the Friendly Isles by Queen Salote of Tonga; spent Christmas in New Zealand, whence she broadcast her annual message to all her peoples; in the New Year made a prolonged tour of Australia which took in the capitals of the Commonwealth and all its six states; passed on to receive the acclamations of Ceylon; brought her royal encouragement to the holders of the imperial outpost at Aden; crossed to Uganda; and then, leaving the *Gothic*, took flight across East and North Africa to the historic battlefield of Tobruk and was at last brought home in the royal yacht *Britannia*, with the Duke of Cornwall and Princess Anne on board, to make a triumphal return up the Thames estuary and drop anchor at last in the Pool of London.

The Queen in the Commonwealth

On these journeys about the Commonwealth and Empire, the object is always essentially the same as in the more limited visits to countries and towns in the British Isles, which have been analysed in an earlier chapter—to enlarge the Queen's range of acquaintance with her subjects and their homes, and give the greatest possible number of people an opportunity to see her and perhaps converse with her. But inasmuch as there are vastly greater distances to cover, and the prospect of the next visit is more remote, it is all the more inevitable that the programme shall be crowded with engagements, to the last disposable minute and to the risk of sheer exhaustion of the central figure.

One labour at least the Queen on her travels is spared: the red boxes of Whitehall do not follow her oversea. They go to the Councillors of State who have been appointed as her deputies in the United Kingdom. Nor are the corresponding state papers of the country she is visiting inflicted upon her: the Governor-General continues to discharge the political business of the monarchy as her representative. She is accompanied most of the way by a member of the Cabinet of the host country as Minister in Attendance, and, if the constitution is federal, probably also by a member of the Government of the state or province through which she is passing. The function of these statesmen is primarily to lend the full weight of Government authority to all the complex organization required to facilitate the smooth progress of the tour; but they are also constantly in the company of the Queen, and are her principal guides and sources of information on every topic, political or social, having to do with the lives of the people.

One object of a royal tour is to give the people visited their fair share of the panoply and pageantry of state ceremonial, by which national pride in a monarchical society is so largely nourished. There are processions through the streets, reviews of troops, state banquets and speeches. If possible, what has been described above as the most solemn royal act after a coronation

187

is repeated in the capitals oversea. That is to say, the political timetable is so adjusted that the opening of a new session coincides with the Queen's visit; and then she opens Parliament in state, with a very close imitation of the ancient ceremonial at Westminster.

The Commons are summoned to the Bar of the Second Chamber if there is one; gold-embroidered state robes are produced for the Speakers; mace-bearers and other functionaries familiar at St. Stephens are in attendance; there is even generally a "Black Rod", in spite of the fact that this is in reality an officer not of Parliament but of the Order of the Garter, to which nothing corresponds in any country outside the United Kingdom. The Speech from the Throne, usually read on her behalf by the Governor-General, is delivered by the Queen, and as in the Mother Country outlines the programme of legislation proposed by the Government for the new session.

The Queen has now carried out this historic ceremony in Ottawa, Wellington, Canberra and Colombo, besides the capitals of several of the Australian states. (The provinces of Canada are in a slightly different constitutional position, and it would not be appropriate for the Queen to open their legislative sessions). It is possible that she will do the same at Accra when she visits Ghana in 1959. And as heiress presumptive she saw Parliaments opened by her father in Cape Town and Salisbury, then the capital of Southern Rhodesia and now of the Central African Federation.

Apart from these state functions, the aim on a royal tour is to move the Queen over the largest area and to introduce her to the greatest number of people, variety of scenery, extent of industry and other characteristic activities that time will permit. She may travel by air, or by a special royal train, according to the nature of the country; occasionally by ship. She often visits three or four towns in the course of a morning. In each the mayor is waiting to receive her with a speech of welcome, to which she makes a speech in reply. Inevitably, all these speeches are very much alike; and the merciful custom has grown up of taking them as read. The manuscripts are exchanged, and the text published afterwards in the local newspaper. Then there is probably a drive to some open space—a public recreation ground or a racecourse—where a dais has been set up and the notable people of the locality are presented to the Queen while the less notable crowd the rails to get a glimpse of her. There is a quick scurry round some model housing estate, factory, or famous beauty spot, and back to the train, ship or aircraft to keep the engagement due in half an hour, ten, twenty or fifty miles away.

Almost every day there is likely to be a more or less formal luncheon in a town hall or other public building, probably with speeches, certainly with many presentations. If there is any important institution lately completed, the Queen will certainly be asked to open it. Some opportunity will have been arranged for the schoolchildren to gather round her, and probably put on some sort of performance for her benefit. Traditional tribal dances or rituals will be enacted before her by Maoris, Ibos, Red Indians, Australian aborigines. She may preside over a Pitso or Indaba as the chief above all chiefs. In more sophisticated places there will often be a Governor's or Administrator's garden party to enable her to meet the leaders of local society, a state banquet, or a royal ball, or several of these things on the same day. Night after night the Queen goes exhausted to bed, counting as she falls asleep the number of mayors, all exactly like the last mayor, to whom she must be polite tomorrow.

But this Queen, as is visible to all who meet her, is buoyed up to meet the endless labour of the royal routine by her deep sense of the importance of the work she is doing and her delight in doing it conscientiously and well. She knows that it is worth while: that she is leaving with every man, woman and child in this bewildering procession that passes before her presence a memory that will endure for a lifetime, and a renewed sense of belonging to a tradition and a fellowship that is greater than they know. Let us take leave of her with a few sentences that the author wrote on her return from the famous journey round the world, and that seem to him, after four years, not to need alteration:

"Each of these far-flung communities which passed on the resounding cry of acclamation from nation to colony and from continent to island round the globe became in that moment more conscious of its kinship to all that came before or after in the endless chain of applause. This idea of a Commonwealth of independent nations held in unbreakable fellowship by the loyalty they share to one personality, honoured and beloved, is an elementary axiom to all who are heirs to the imperial tradition. What the Commonwealth Tour has done is to demonstrate the truth of the axiom to those who have not the birthright and might have doubted; for Her Majesty has voyaged under the eyes, not uniformly friendly, of a watching world. Two things above all have been shown to these outside observers: first, that the same institutions of free self-government can flourish in lands differing widely in race, language, faith and history; secondly, that the bonds that link them together are engendered in their own hearts, not imposed upon them from above. These things, which cannot be doubted by friend or foe who has been permitted to see the events of the Tour undistorted, will have their influence upon the future of the world.

"The shares of the Queen and her subjects in the great achievement cannot be wholly separated, for it is the way of the Commonwealth that its kings and queens and their peoples make their history in collaboration. But it must be said that the triumph would have been less if the Queen had shown herself other than she is. It was no hieratic image of abstract royalty that moved among her people, but a human being to be honoured and loved for her own qualities—her dignity, her grace, her instant sympathy with all sorts and conditions, her unremitting application to the endless labours required of her, but perhaps most of all the sense of joy that radiated from her, the joy that comes of the consciousness of a great mission worthily performed at whatever cost in personal exhaustion, the same joy that shone in her eyes as she sat enthroned in Westminster Abbey, and which seems to sustain her always and communicate itself to all who serve her closely.

"She has returned to England something more than the Queen who flew across the Atlantic on that November day. The neophyte phase of the reign is over; she moves with a new confidence and authority. Already her experience begins to be unique. No one else, in the whole Commonwealth and Empire, has been taken so close to the hearts of all its peoples, and at the same time shared the confidence of so many of its leaders in considering the problems and hopes of the nations committed, under her, to their charge.

"As the years pass this special quality in her experience will grow more pronounced, set her in one sense more apart from all other living men and women, yet in another unite her more intimately to her own. Of her statesmen throughout the Commonwealth some will fall from power and some will leave the stage for ever; but she will still be in her place. All her Ministers, everywhere, have their vision limited by the particular national horizon within which their commission to serve her is held. She alone has the duty, and the opportunity, to see the Commonwealth steadily and see it whole. And in the deepest sense it is only through the existence of at least one mind that can thus comprehend it as a whole that the unity of the Commonwealth itself becomes an objective reality and not a figure of rhetoric."